CONTEMPORARY'S
READY, SET, STUDY!
Improving Your Study Skills

WENDY STEIN

Project Editor
Mark Boone

CB

CONTEMPORARY
BOOKS

CHICAGO

Published by Contemporary Books, Inc.
180 North Michigan Avenue, Chicago, Illinois 60601
Manufactured in the United States of America
International Standard Book Number: 0-8092-4267-2

Published simultaneously in Canada by
Fitzhenry & Whiteside
91 Granton Drive
Richmond Hill, Ontario L4B 2N5
Canada

Editorial Director Caren Van Slyke	*Cover Design* Lois Koehler
Editorial Sarah Schmidt Betsy Rubin Jane Samuelson Robin O'Connor Lynn McEwan Lisa Dillman	*Illustrators* Daniel J. Hochstatter Rosemary Morrissey-Herzberg *Art & Production* Princess Louise El Jan Geist
Editorial Production Manager Norma Fioretti	*Typography* Terrence Alan Stone
Production Editor Craig Bolt	*Graphics* J•B Typesetting St. Charles, Illinois

Cover photo © C. C. Cain Photography

Dedicated to our friend, Pat Reid

Contents

Acknowledgments   v

Introduction   1

1 Getting Motivated   2
Getting in Shape   4
Setting Long-Term Goals   5
Setting Short-Term Goals   6
Managing Your Time   7
Chapter Review   8

2 Using Textbooks   9
Using the Table of Contents   10
Locating Chapter Heads and Subheads   11
Finding Keys Words and the Glossary   12
Understanding an Index   14
Using Introductions, Summaries, and Study Questions   16
Chapter Review   18

3 Reading Visual Aids   20
Reading Bar Graphs   21
Reading Line Graphs   24
Reading Circle Graphs   26
Reading Charts   29
Interpreting Maps   32
More on Interpreting Maps   34
Reading Time Lines   35
Understanding Editorial Cartoons   37
Chapter Review   40

4 Reading Strategies   42
Previewing   43
Skimming   46
Scanning   48
Following the SQ3R Method   50
Note Taking   52
Drawing Thought Webs   54
Using Memory Aids   56
Improving Listening Skills   58
Chapter Review   59

5 Using Reference Tools   61
Putting Words in Alphabetical Order   62
Using Guide Words in the Dictionary   64

Improving Spelling and Hyphenation   66
Looking Up Word Meanings   68
Using Pronunciation Keys   71
Looking Up Word Origins   72
Choosing Words in a Thesaurus   73
Doing Research from an Encyclopedia   76
Researching Magazine Articles   79
Using the Library   81
Finding a Book in the Stacks   85
Chapter Review   86

6 Writing Research Papers   89
Following Writing Steps   90
Taking Notes with Note Cards   92
Developing an Outline   93
Getting Organized   95
Completing Bibliography Cards   97
Chapter Review   98

7 A Winning Attitude   100
Getting Ready   101
Studying for a Test   102
Starting the Test   104
Answering True-False Questions   106
Answering Multiple-Choice Questions   108
Taking Matching Tests   111
Fill-in-the-Blank Questions   112
Planning for Essay Tests   114
Answering Essay Test Questions   117
The Successful Student: Cramming vs. Studying   120
Chapter Review   121

Answer Key   123

Acknowledgments

We gratefully acknowledge those who have granted us permission to reprint the following:

Time line on page 36—"U.S. Presidents: 1889–1939"—from CHARTS ON FILE, by The Diagram Group. Copyright © 1988 by The Diagram Group. Reprinted with the permission of Facts on File, Inc., New York, NY.

Cartoon on page 38 by Jeff MacNelly. Reprinted by permission: Tribune Media Services.

Cartoon on page 39 by EWK, © 1989 Cartoonists and Writers Syndicate.

Dictionary entries on pages 69 and 87 from *Webster's New World Dictionary of the American Language, Third College Edition*, © 1988. Used by permission of the publisher, Simon & Schuster, Inc., New York, NY.

Thesaurus entries on pages 73 and 74 from *The New American Roget's College Thesaurus in Dictionary Form*, © 1962. Used by permission of the New American Library.

Thesaurus entries on pages 74 and 75 from *Roget's International Thesaurus*, 4th edition. Copyright © 1977 by Harper and Row Publishers, Inc. Reprinted by permission of Harper and Row Publishers, Inc.

Encyclopedia entries on pages 77 and 78 from *The World Book Encyclopedia*. © 1989 World Book, Inc. By permission of the publisher.

Entries on pages 79 and 87 from *Reader's Guide to Periodical Literature*, February 1989, vol. 88, no. 17. Copyright © 1989 by the H. W. Wilson Company. Material reproduced with permission of the publisher.

Sterling Bicycle on cover distributed by Lawee, Inc. Reproduced by permission.

Velotech Cycling Gloves on cover manufactured and distributed exclusively by Cycles Peugeot, Carlstadt, N.J. Reproduced by permission.

Lake Sport Cycling Shoes on cover manufactured exclusively by Look America Corporation. Reproduced by permission.

The editor has made every effort to trace the ownership of all copyrighted material, and necessary permissions have been secured in most cases. Should there prove to be a question regarding the use of any material, regret is hereby expressed for such error. Upon notification of any such oversight, proper acknowledgment will be made in future editions.

CONTEMPORARY'S

READY, SET, STUDY!

Introduction

On your mark . . . get ready . . . set . . . GO!

The firing of a starting pistol signals the beginning of a race. However, the real beginning of a race involves the preparation that the athlete must undergo in order to compete. What the athlete does to get in shape often spells the difference between victory and defeat.

Likewise, in order for you to perform at your best in school, you will need to condition yourself mentally and physically much like successful athletes do. You will need to set achievable goals, organize yourself, plan your study time, and discipline yourself to study if you want to succeed.

Ready, Set, Study! will help you in your task of improving the study skills that are so necessary for your success in the classroom. Some of these important skills include getting motivated, managing your time, understanding how to use reference tools, learning ways to help make writing research papers easier, and getting ready to take tests.

Throughout this book, you will find many features designed to help you strengthen your study skills. They include:

- cartoons that open each chapter, introducing the topic

- activities that encourage you to examine your own habits and set goals

- study tips that you can put to use immediately to improve your skills

- checklists that help you see how often you apply the tips you've learned

- chapter reviews that allow you to check your understanding of the material you've read

- "do it yourself" activities that enable you to apply ideas you've learned

- challenge questions that give you a chance to test your knowledge

Most of all, *Ready, Set, Study!* is an *active* book. This means that you learn the skills contained in it by *doing*, by putting them into practice as often as you can.

You'll be surprised at how much the new skills that you learn can help you to perform better in school. Go for it!

Chapter 1

Getting Motivated

Are you about to get a pep talk? Well, yes ... but pep talks work because they help you to do your best. In this chapter, you will learn skills that will improve your ability to perform your best in school.

What do you say to yourself when you are confronted with a new task? Do you say, "I can do it. I can learn"? Or do you immediately say to yourself, "I can't do it. I've never done it, so I don't know how"?

Think of what an athlete does before playing a sport. An athlete goes into training. That's what you have to do to become a more successful student—go into training with new study habits. What are the elements of any kind of training program?

■ Getting in shape

■ Managing your time

■ Setting short-term goals

■ Setting long-term goals

You'll learn more about these skills in this chapter. The first step, however, is to get motivated.

Pep talks have a big effect on your self-confidence and your ability to learn new things. Positive messages fill you with enthusiasm and energy. When you believe in yourself, you have the confidence to try new things, to take chances—to learn. Negative messages drain you of confidence and energy. As a result, you are less willing to take chances.

Try this exercise with other people in your class or with a tape recorder by yourself.

■ Repeat "I *can* learn, I *can* succeed" over and over again while classmates or a tape recording repeats "You *can't,* you *can't,* you *can't.*"

■ Now repeat "I *can* learn, I *can* succeed" over and over again while classmates or the tape recording repeats "You *can* do it, you *can* do it, you *can* do it."

How did you feel when the voices said "you *can*"? How did you feel when they said "you *can't*"? Did you feel encouraged when they said "you *can*"? Did you feel discouraged when they said "you *can't*"?

If you are listening to negative tapes, it's time to change the message to "I *can* learn good study skills. I *want* to learn good study skills. I am *open* to learning good study skills."

Learning the skills in this book will enable you to be a better student. These skills will be useful to you for the rest of your life. If you master even one new skill from this book, you will be successful because that is one thing you hadn't mastered before. Mastering a new skill feels good. Imagine your sense of accomplishment when you actually use what you have learned. Think about how good you'll feel when you can teach it to someone else. Learn a new skill and pass on your knowledge to your parents, a brother or sister, another student. You'll feel great.

Words You'll Need to Know

These important words will be used in Chapter 1. Read what each word means.

motivate—to give one the impulse to do something
goal—what a person is aiming toward
schedule—a plan that shows time set aside for certain activities

Getting in Shape

Mind and body must be in shape if you are going to live and study at your best. By following the tips below, you can improve your ability to study.

■ Food is fuel. When you put bad gasoline in your car, the car runs poorly. You run poorly on the wrong fuel too. Snack on healthy foods when you are studying. Don't study right after you eat a full meal. You are likely to be drowsy then, since much of your blood supply is working on digestion rather than going to your brain!

■ Get enough sleep. Most people need between six and eight hours of sleep a night. If you have a hard time staying awake to study, it might be because you are not getting enough sleep.

■ For best concentration, sit up when you study. Try to find a time and place where there are few distractions. Be sure you have the materials you need on hand before you start.

■ If you feel like getting up and moving around every half hour or so, don't be too surprised. Humans are built to move around at least every half hour.

■ If your eyes get tired, try "eye cupping." If you wear glasses, take them off. Close your eyes and put your elbows on the desk or table. Let the weight of your head fall into the palms of your hands so that your hands are cupped over your eye sockets. Rest for a minute or so. Take long, deep breaths. You'll feel refreshed.

PRACTICE

Directions: Here are some questions about keeping in shape. Answer each question with a brief statement.

1. What time do you go to bed at night? _____

2. What time do you wake up? _____

3. Are you alert for work or for school? _____

4. Do you think you get enough rest? _____

5. List three things that you can do to become more alert when studying. _____

_____

STUDY TIP: Be your own biggest fan! Cheer yourself on. Give yourself positive messages. Take good care of your mind and body.

Setting Long-Term Goals

Now take some time to look at your **goals** for studying. People perform better if they can see how their activities relate to their goals. Do you know what you want to do when you get out of school? What are your dreams? These are your long-term goals. List some of them in the left-hand column below. Then, in the right-hand column, write what action you can take to achieve each one that you list. One is done for you.

Long-Term Goals	Actions to Achieve Them
1. *have my own apartment*	1. *get a job that pays a good salary*
2.	2.
3.	3.
4.	4.
5.	5.

Now compare your lists with other students' lists. You might want to add some goals to your list. These two lists are your motivation, your driving force, for being in school and studying. In short, they are your reasons for learning.

STUDY TIP: Write your immediate goal on a posterboard and post it in a place where you can see it each day.

Setting Short-Term Goals

A Chinese proverb says, "A journey of 1,000 miles begins with one step." Keep your mind on your goal, and know that as you study and attend classes, you are making steady progress.

What are some of your study goals for the next few weeks and months? What do you need or want to get done soon? These are your short-term goals.

► List some of them in the left-hand column below; then in the right-hand column, write what action you can take to achieve each one that you list. One is done for you.

Short-Term Study Goals	Actions to Achieve Them
1. *to take computer programming II next term*	1. *work hard to pass computer programming I*
2.	2.
3.	3.
4.	4.
5.	5.

Now choose the most important goal from the list above and write the steps that are required for you to reach that goal.

Goal: _____

Step 1. _____

Step 2. _____

Step 3. _____

> **STUDY TIP:** List your short-term goals for each class at the beginning of each term. Then list the steps that you need to follow to realize each goal.

Managing Your Time

Select a regular time for homework and studying. Make an agreement with yourself, a commitment, to do your work then. Decide to really work during that time. Below is a **schedule** that you can use to plan your study time.

■ First, block out the hours that you must spend at classes, work, and other activities. Write the name of each activity and the time it starts.

■ Next, block out the hours that you would like to set aside for family, friends, and yourself. Write a label for each block of time such as *Family, Friends,* or *Personal.*

■ Finally, decide when would be the best time to study each day. Block out those hours on the schedule. Write *Study* in each block of time; then, with a colored pencil, lightly color in the blocks of time.

Study Schedule

	Monday	Tuesday	Wednesday	Thursday	Friday	Saturday	Sunday
8 AM							
9 AM							
10 AM							
11 AM							
12 PM							
1 PM							
2 PM							
3 PM							
4 PM							
5 PM							
6 PM							
7 PM							
8 PM							
9 PM							
10 PM							

Chapter Review

Comprehension Check

Directions: Show how much you learned in Chapter 1. Circle the letter that shows the correct answer. Some questions have more than one correct answer.

1. What can you do to motivate yourself to study?
   a. compete with other students
   b. repeat positive messages to yourself
   c. focus on your failures so as not to repeat the same mistakes

2. What can you do to improve your ability to study?
   a. study right after you eat
   b. study while lying down in bed
   c. listen to a Walkman when studying
   d. take periodic rest breaks

3. What is a long-term goal?
   a. a goal that you can achieve in a month
   b. a goal that a teacher sets for you
   c. a goal that you hope to realize later in life

4. What is a short-term goal?
   a. a goal that you can realize in a matter of weeks or months
   b. a strategy for winning a football game
   c. a goal that is not so important to accomplish

5. Why is a schedule helpful?
   a. it helps you to remember the courses you have
   b. it helps you to plan the time you need to study
   c. it is a handy way of checking your long-term goals

Chapter 2
Using Textbooks

If you study a directory in a store before you begin to shop, you are less likely to waste time trying to find the various departments. Much like a store's directory, every book has a "map" to guide you. Let's look at some important features of a book's map. These include the table of contents, chapter heads and subheads, key words and glossaries, indexes, introductions, summaries, and study questions.

Words You'll Need to Know

These important words will be used in Chapter 2. Read what each word means.

glossary—a short dictionary of terms used in a book

heading—a title that appears at the top of a chapter or section; it tells the topic you'll read about

index—an alphabetical listing of a book's important topics that is found at the back

key words—words that are especially important to a topic of study

summary—a brief explanation of the highlights of a chapter

table of contents—a listing of a book's chapters and topics that is found at the front

Using the Table of Contents

The table of contents is one of the most helpful items in the front of the book. It is a guide that tells you:

- what the book contains

- the pages on which to find this information

The table of contents is also an outline of the book that shows how the book is organized. Is the book broken up into units or parts, chapters, or lessons? What are the major topics in the book? By answering these questions about the table of contents, you get an overview of the entire book. The title of the following book is *Creative Clowning*. Look at its table of contents below.

Chapter **1. What Is a Clown?**...................9
  Traditions of Clowning • Theater • Famous Clowns

Chapter **2. What Kind of Clown Are You?**....................22
  Clown Types • Developing a Character • What to Wear? • Clown Face Makeup

Chapter **3. Clown Tricks**....................45
  Using Balloons • Squirt Guns • Walking Tall on Stilts • Juggling • Magic • Unicycling

Chapter **4. Jobs for Clowns**....................72
  Carnivals • Birthday Parties • The Circus • Workshops • Finding Work

PRACTICE

Directions: Use the table of contents above to answer questions about the book.

1. What is the title of Chapter 1? _____

2. On what page does Chapter 2 begin? _____

3. On what page does Chapter 3 begin? _____

4. In what chapter (number and name) will you find information on the history of clowning? _____

5. In what chapter will you learn about walking on stilts? _____ On what page does the chapter begin? _____

Locating Chapter Heads and Subheads

After you look through a book's table of contents, you should turn to the text itself. You'll find that it is arranged so that you can find topics easily. Each **heading** is a clue to help you find the main point of the section. Each heading also lets you know that either a new topic or new information is being introduced. Headings help you focus your reading and locate information. Look at the page below:

The *chapter head* and number are in the largest print on the page. They may even be in a different color.	

5
U.S. HISTORY

"Those who cannot remember the past are condemned to repeat it," said the philosopher George Santayana. Was he right?

World War I was supposed to be "the war to end all wars," but of course, it was not. Twenty-one years after it ended, World War II began.

A no-win situation in a limited, undeclared war in Korea apparently was not reminder enough to keep the U.S. from becoming involved in Vietnam.

We study history to help chart our future by studying the past. Sometimes we learn from our mistakes, but many times we do not. In this chapter, you will study U.S. History. As you read, try to keep in mind events today that parallel those of yesterday. You may find that, indeed, history repeats itself.

Subheads break the chapter into smaller parts. They are either larger, **bolder**, in a different color, or in a different style of type. They tell you the main topic of the section.

A New Nation in a New World

Exploration, Discovery, and Colonization

In some ways Christopher Columbus can be considered a failure. He originally set sail in 1492 to find a new, easier passage to the Far East to make trade

Sometimes there are even smaller headings or topics that focus on details within a section.

PRACTICE

Directions: Use your social studies, history, literature, and science textbooks for this exercise. For two of the books, write the chapter title and the next level of subheads in the spaces below. Do you see that the subheads are the main topics to study in the chapter?

Book title: _____   Book title: _____

Chapter 1 head: _____   Chapter 1 head: _____

Subheads: _____   Subheads: _____

_____   _____

_____   _____

STUDY TIP: By reading chapter heads and subheads first, you'll get a preview of what a chapter is about before you start reading.

Finding Key Words and the Glossary

As you read, you may find that some words are in **bold** or *italic* print. They are usually **key words**. They have special importance to the topic. They are usually defined in the text.

The following paragraph shows how key words are used:

> The U.S. Constitution promises that a person accused of a crime will have a fair trial. The accused, or **defendant**, is entitled to a lawyer. He or she is also entitled to a trial by **jury**. A jury is a group of citizens who decide the defendant's guilt or innocence.

▶ What are the key words in the paragraph? _____

Answer: *defendant* and *jury*

Key words and other words may also be grouped in a **glossary**. The glossary may be at the back of the book and include words from the entire book, or it may appear after each chapter. The words in a glossary are listed in alphabetical order as words are in a dictionary.

Here's a glossary that you might find in a book about the U.S. legal system:

---

acquit—to find the *defendant* not guilty of a crime
allege—to assert without proof
appeal—a request that a higher court review a court decision
arson—unlawfully setting fire to property
bail—money paid to the court to release a *defendant* from jail until the trial is over
convict—to find a defendant guilty of a crime
defendant—the person accused of wrongdoing
felony—a major crime such as murder or rape
indict—to formally charge with a crime
jury—a group of citizens who give a *verdict* in court
misdemeanor—a minor crime such as a traffic violation
perjury—telling a lie to the court
plaintiff—the person who formally accuses another of wrongdoing
prosecute—to carry out a case against a *defendant*
subpoena—a written order telling a person to appear in court to *testify*
summons—a written order to appear in court
testify—to tell what you know about a case in court
verdict—the decision of the court

PRACTICE

Directions: Answer the following questions based on the glossary on page 12.

1. What is the glossary definition of *jury*? _____

_____

2. How is a *subpoena* different from a *summons*? _____

_____

3. How does a *felony* differ from a *misdemeanor*? _____

_____

4. Which two people in a lawsuit oppose one another? _____

_____

MORE PRACTICE

Directions: Pick out the key words in each selection below. Figure out the meaning of each word from the context of the selection and write a definition. Then check the definitions you have written. Be sure that the ideas are the same.

1. A person accused of a crime is considered innocent until proven guilty. Unless the crime is very serious and the accused has been in trouble before, he or she is usually released on **bail**. The bail money is meant to ensure that the defendant does not run away before the trial begins.

_____

2. The court sends a **subpoena** to each witness. The witness must appear in court to **testify**. The defendant's lawyer and the prosecutor ask the witness questions. The jury listens to all the witnesses before it makes its decision.

_____

_____

3. The jury has two choices. It can either find the defendant guilty, or it can **acquit** him or her.

_____

4. The job of state's attorney is to **prosecute** a person who has committed a crime against the state.

_____

STUDY TIP: You can remember unfamiliar words more easily if you write down their definitions. Get a notebook and letter the pages A–Z. Make your own glossary of unfamiliar words as you read new material.

Understanding an Index

At the back of most textbooks and other nonfiction books, there is an alphabetical listing of the important topics in the book. This is followed by the page numbers on which you'll find information about the topics. This listing is called an **index**. An index guides you to the information quickly. You don't have to page through the book looking for the information if you have an index.

You might find an index like this for a book on computers:

A
abacus, 3
adding machines, 5–6
Apple Computers, 100, 105
Asimov, Isaac, 10–11

B
BASIC, 72, 80–82, 91
binary code, 33, 37
bit, 45, 51
bug, 66
byte, 45, 52

C
cathode ray tube (CRT), 99
Central Processing Unit (CPU) 81–82
COBOL, 41
CRT, (*See* cathode ray tube)

D
data, 56–57, 74
disks, floppy, 32–34, 71;
  hard, 33–34, 88–90

To find information, look up the word or topic you are interested in. After the word, page numbers are listed. A dash (–) between numbers means *to* (from page 35 *to* page 37). A *comma* (,) between numbers in an entry means *and*.

▶ On what pages will you find information about floppy disks?

_____

Answer: pages 32–34 and 71

Sometimes you will not find the entry under the first word of a phrase. *Hard disk* was indexed under *D* for disk, not *h* for hard. The index may refer you to the correct entry, or you may have to try another entry by looking at the second word. People's names are listed under the first letter of the last name. If you are looking up a title that begins with an article such as *a* or *the*, look up the second word of the title.

▶ Under what letter will you find *Isaac Asimov*? ____ On what pages will you find information about this science fiction writer?

_____

Answers: A; pages 10–11

PRACTICE

Directions: Use the index on the facing page to answer these questions:

1. On what page(s) will you find information about bits? _____

2. On what page(s) will you find information about bytes? _____

3. On what page(s) will you find information about the CRT? _____ Under what entry did you find the information? _____

4. Are you likely to find information about computer dating in this book? _____

5. Are you likely to find information about Apple Computers in this book? _____ Atari computers? _____

MORE PRACTICE

Directions: What word do you think would be your *best* bet to look up in order to find each of these items in an index? Write your answer next to the phrase or name. Answers can vary.

1. Eleanor Roosevelt _____

2. United States of America _____

3. Soviet Union _____

4. Department of Transportation _____

5. Supreme Court _____

6. United Nations _____

7. World War II _____

Using Your Skills

Sometimes an entry has several topics in it. Decide what word (or words) you would look up in an index of a book of general information to find out about these subjects.

8. the election of Andrew Jackson _____

9. the attack on Pearl Harbor _____

10. differences between Asian and African elephants _____

11. the year the Empire State Building was finished _____

12. the star of the "I Love Lucy" show _____

STUDY TIP: To find a word in an index, think about what the most important word in the entry is. Look up that word first.

Using Introductions, Summaries, and Study Questions

Many textbooks have *introductions* to the book, to the unit, or to each of the chapters. Introductions are previews of what is to come in the text. The introduction tells you what is important to think about as you read. Some introductions to books include chapter *objectives*, or *goals*. A chapter objective tells you what you are expected to learn after studying a chapter. For example, objectives included in a science textbook's chapter about scientific investigation might be:

- You will learn the six steps of the scientific method.

- You will learn how to apply these steps in an experiment.

- You will learn how to use controls to ensure that your experiment is free from bias.

Some books have chapter **summaries** at the end of each chapter. The summaries give you the highlights—the most important information contained in a chapter. Look through this book to see if there is a section that appears at the beginning or end of each chapter.

Also, at the beginning or end of some chapters are *study questions*. These questions give you a purpose for reading. As you read, you will be looking for answers to those questions.

PRACTICE

Directions: A chapter or unit summary may have a special name. Put a ☑ next to the terms below that might signal to you that you are reading a summary.

____ **a.** Chapter review

____ **b.** Chapter outline

____ **c.** A Look Back

____ **d.** Exercises

____ **e.** Glossary of Terms

____ **f.** Remember This . . .

____ **g.** Practicing your skills

____ **h.** In Summary . . .

____ **i.** Summing Up . . .

____ **j.** Practical Living Skills

____ **k.** Chapter Preview

Do It Yourself

Directions: Choose two of your textbooks and put a check ☑ next to the items that are featured in each of them.

Title of book _____

____ Book introduction

____ Unit introductions

____ Chapter introductions

____ Chapter summary or review

What summary or review is called _____

____ Study questions

____ Chapter objectives or goals

____ Glossary

____ Index

Title of book _____

____ Book introduction

____ Unit introductions

____ Chapter introductions

____ Chapter summary or review

What summary or review is called _____

____ Study questions

____ Chapter objectives or goals

____ Glossary

____ Index

> **STUDY TIP:** Always read the summary when you finish reading the chapter—even if you are sure you've understood everything. The summary helps you pull together all of the important information in the chapter.

Chapter Review

Comprehension Check

Show how much you learned in Chapter 2. Complete these exercises.

Finding Your Way

Directions: Put in order the following steps for becoming familiar with a book. Write the number 1 for the first step, 2 for the second, and so on.

_____ Skim the table of contents for organization and topics.

_____ Look through the text for chapter headings and subheads.

_____ Look for and read any chapter introductions.

_____ Look for study questions following the text.

_____ Read the text and all picture captions.

Table of Contents

Directions: Using the following table of contents from a health textbook, answer the questions on the next page.

Chapter		Page
1	Exercise for Fitness	3
2	Eat Right	17
3	Your Weight	29
4	Teeth	37
5	A Good Night's Sleep	45
6	Know Your Emotions	49

For each subject below, write the number of the chapter in which you would be likely to find the information.

1. Dealing with anger ____

2. The dangers of too much salt ____

3. How much you should weigh ____

4. The four food groups ____

Index

Directions: Using the following index from a book about home construction, answer the questions below. Note: "f" after a number means there is an illustration. Numbers listed in **dark** type mean that the entire chapter is devoted to the topic.

> **U**
> Unit rise, 125, 127; (*see also* Riser)
>
> **V**
> Vapor barrier, 183–185; (*see also* Insulation)
> Ventilation, and attic, 224, 225f
> Vise grips, 112, 112f
>
> **W**
> Windows, **74–88**; installing, 74–80; leveling, 74–75; trimming, 80–84
> Woods, grains of, 190f; hardwood, 190–191; softwood, 191–192

1. On what page would you find an illustration of vise grips? _____

2. What other word would you look up to find information on unit rise? _____

3. On what pages would you find information on the grains of softwoods? _____

4. What other word can you look up to find out about vapor barriers? _____

5. Which subject covers an entire chapter? _____

6. For what three topics are illustrations provided? _____

7. Oak is considered a hardwood. On what page(s) would information about oak be covered? _____

8. Pine is considered a softwood. On what page(s) would information about pine be covered? _____

Chapter 3
Reading Visual Aids

Meteorologists depend on visual aids—maps, charts, and graphs—to help them forecast the weather or show temperature ranges. Photographs, illustrations, and graphs make your books more interesting. They break up the text. They also present important information in a visual format to help you understand it better.

Words You'll Need to Know

These important words will be used in Chapter 3. Read what each word means.

data—factual information

horizontal axis—the line along the bottom of a graph that shows the values being compared

legend—a list of symbols on a map or chart including their explanations

vertical axis—the line along the left side of a graph that shows the values being compared

trend—the direction that a line shows on a graph over a period of time

Reading Bar Graphs

Bar graphs are a clear and easy way to present information. You can see differences and changes at a glance.

A bar graph often compares two or more sets of information. The graph might compare countries, men and women, or even men with flat feet and men with high arches. On a bar graph the bars can be shown horizontally or vertically. Look at the graph below. The bars are drawn *horizontally*.

To understand this graph, follow these steps:

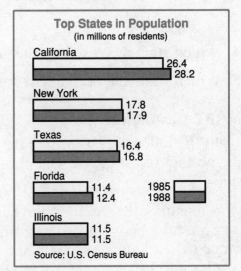

1. **Read the title.** It tells the topic of the graph. This graph shows the states that are highest in population. The numbers stand for

   _____.

2. **Look for information near the bars.** On this graph, the names of the _____ are written above the bars. The population numbers in millions are written on the right side.

3. **Look at the key.** It tells what each of the bars stands for. In this graph, the white bar stands for _____ population figures. The shaded bar stands for _____ population. Now you know that populations in the years _____ are being compared.

4. **Look at the information in small print at the bottom.** It tells the source (where the information came from). The information in the graph came from the _____.

5. **Look for answers to specific questions to make sure you understand the graph.** Ask yourself: Which state had the greatest population in 1988? _____ What was its population that year? _____

Answers: 1. millions **2.** states **3.** 1985; 1988; 1985 and 1988 **4.** U.S. Census Bureau **5.** California; 28.2 million

PRACTICE

Directions: Refer to the graph on page 21 to answer these questions.

1. What five states had the highest populations in the United States in 1988? _____

   _____

2. What was the third most populated state in 1985? _____ In 1988? _____

3. Did the order of the most populated states change between 1985 and 1988? If

   so, how? _____

   _____

4. Which state increased by the greatest number of residents? _____

5. Which state had no increase? _____

MORE PRACTICE

In the following bar graph, the years being compared are represented along the bottom of the graph. The number of people (population) is shown along the side.

Sometimes the length of the bars on a graph falls between two numbers. In order to read such graphs accurately, you have to **estimate** the correct number lying between the values. For example, on this graph (showing persons living alone, by sex) the number of men living alone in 1970 falls between 3 million and 4 million. Since the number would be more than 3 million and less than 4 million we can estimate it to be about 3.5 million.

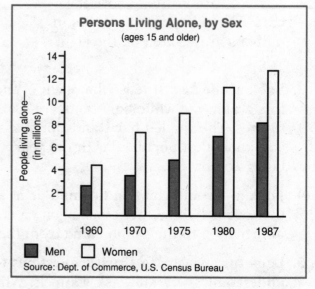

Directions: Look at the graph and answer the following questions:

1. What years are being compared? _____

2. a. What does the shaded bar stand for? _____

   b. What does the white bar stand for? _____

3. What information is given along the left side of the graph? Along the bottom of the graph?

   _____

   _____

4. a. Has the number of women living alone gone up or down since 1960? _____

b. Has the number of men living alone gone up or down since 1960? _____

5. Do more men than women live alone? _____

6. a. About how many women lived alone in 1980? _____

b. About how many men lived alone in 1980? _____

Challenge

Why do you think more women than men live alone? _____

_____

_____

Do It Yourself

Create your own bar graph. Use the information on the right that shows the popular vote totals for major-party candidates in presidential elections from 1976 to 1988. (The numbers are rounded off to the nearest million votes.)

	Republican	Democrat
1976	39 million	41 million
1980	44 million	35 million
1984	54 million	37 million
1988	48 million	41 million

1. Write the title above the graph.

2. Label the vertical axis "Votes (in millions)." Label the slash marks for every two million—from 38 to 54 million.

3. Label the horizontal axis "Years." Label the slash marks for each of the four election years.

4. Draw bars based on the data above. Shade the bars that stand for the Republican Party votes; do not shade the bars that stand for the Democratic Party votes.

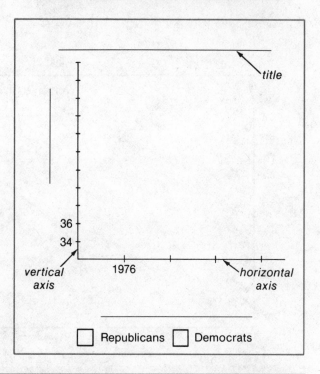

STUDY TIP: To understand how to read a bar graph, read the title and the information along the side and bottom of the graph, and ask yourself specific questions about the graph.

Reading Line Graphs

Now that you're familiar with bar graphs, understanding line graphs should be easier. Line graphs quickly show highs, lows, and the degree of change over a time period.

Time periods are usually displayed across the **horizontal axis** on bar and line graphs. Amount is shown along the **vertical axis**. The line on the graph can move up or down or remain level for a period of time. A direction that a line shows on a graph is called a **trend**. Upward movement of the line indicates an increase. Downward movement indicates a decrease. A line that is level indicates little or no change.

Shown below is a graph that indicates the winning heights of the women's Olympic high jump. Along the horizontal axis are the years that the Olympic Games were held. The vertical axis shows the heights jumped. As you can see, there was quite an increase in the winning height over the course of sixty years.

▶ How high did the winner jump in 1984? _____ Look at the year at the bottom. Look at the heights at the side. Follow the year up to the height.

Answer: The winner jumped between 6'6" and 6'8".

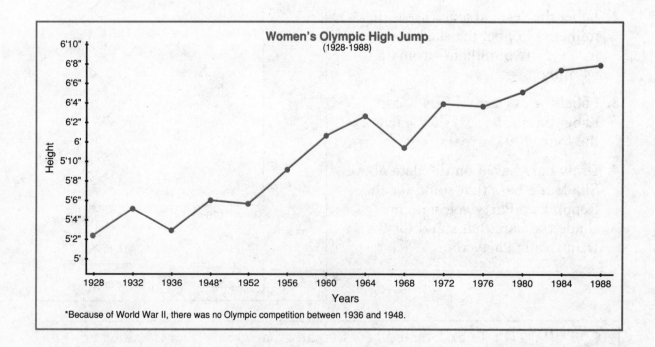

*Because of World War II, there was no Olympic competition between 1936 and 1948.

PRACTICE

Directions: Use the Women's Olympic High Jump graph to answer these questions. You may have to use information you already know to answer one of the questions. Write T for true or F for false.

_____ **1.** Since 1928, there has been a downward trend in jumping heights.

_____ **2.** There was a decrease in jumping height between 1932 and 1936.

_____ **3.** The 1988 winner jumped almost one and one-half feet higher than the 1928 winner.

_____ **4.** The vertical axis is marked off in one-foot increments.

_____ **5.** Generally the Olympic Games are held during the same year as the U.S. presidential election.

_____ **6.** Since 1928, the Olympic Games have been held every four years without interruption.

> **STUDY TIP:** A line graph shows changes over time. A brief glance can tell you if there has been a rise or fall or steady, straight-line progress.

Reading Circle Graphs

In a circle, or pie, graph, the circle is cut into wedges to show the different size shares that make up the whole. The wedges add up to 100 percent. Circle graphs are often used to show budgets—how money is spent.

By now you're a pro at reading graphs. To read circle graphs, follow these steps:

■ **Read the title.** What is the graph showing? Read any other special notes or subheads. They might tell what time period the graph covers, or what the circle adds up to in dollars.

■ **Note the unit of measurement.** Is the pie cut up into amounts of money (thousands, billions, hundreds)? Is it cut up into percentages to add up to 100 percent? Is it cut up into a fixed period of time (twenty-four hours/one day)?

■ **Note the categories being measured.** Does the pie show groups of people, activities, budget items?

■ **Note the source of the information that provided the numbers.**

■ **Ask yourself specific questions about the graph to help you understand it.** For example, who gets the biggest piece of the pie?

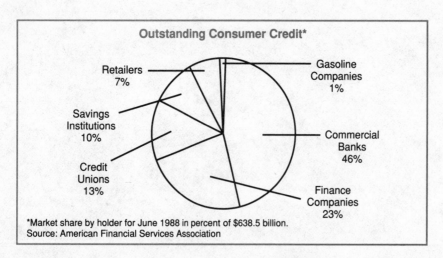

Outstanding Consumer Credit*

Retailers 7%
Gasoline Companies 1%
Savings Institutions 10%
Commercial Banks 46%
Credit Unions 13%
Finance Companies 23%

*Market share by holder for June 1988 in percent of $638.5 billion.
Source: American Financial Services Association

► What does this graph show? _____

_____

Answer: The graph compares how much credit consumers owe to different financial institutions.

PRACTICE

Directions: Use the circle graph on page 26 to answer these questions.

1. What is the total amount of the pie in dollars? _____

_____

2. Where did this information come from? _____

_____

3. What percentage of outstanding consumer credit is owed to each of these markets?

   a. Retailers _____

   b. Gasoline companies _____

   c. Credit unions _____

   d. Finance companies _____

   e. Savings institutions _____

4. **a.** What financial market lends the most money to consumers?

   _____

   b. What is its market share? _____

   _____

5. What financial market lends the least money to consumers? _____

Challenge

How could you figure out how many actual *dollars* consumers owe to each of

these markets? _____

_____

> **S**TUDY TIP: Remember that a circle graph must always add up to 100% or a total amount.

MORE PRACTICE

Directions: Use the graph to answer the questions below.

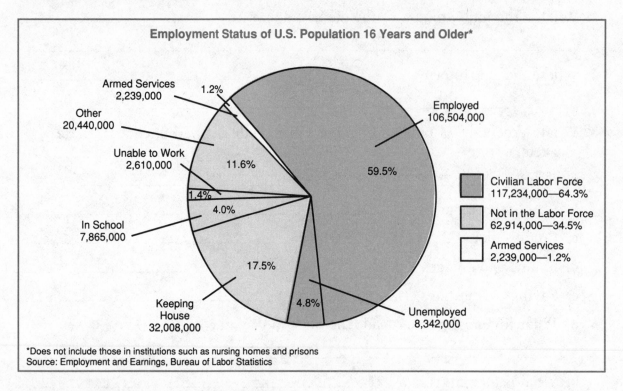

Employment Status of U.S. Population 16 Years and Older*

Armed Services 2,239,000 — 1.2%

Other 20,440,000 — 11.6%

Employed 106,504,000 — 59.5%

Unable to Work 2,610,000 — 1.4%

4.0%

In School 7,865,000

Keeping House 32,008,000 — 17.5%

4.8%

Unemployed 8,342,000

Civilian Labor Force 117,234,000—64.3%

Not in the Labor Force 62,914,000—34.5%

Armed Services 2,239,000—1.2%

*Does not include those in institutions such as nursing homes and prisons
Source: Employment and Earnings, Bureau of Labor Statistics

1. What is the subject of this graph? _____

_____

2. What percentage of the population over sixteen years old was employed in the

   year the graph shows? ____

3. **a.** How many people served in the armed forces? _____

   b. What percentage of the circle is that? ____

4. What percentage of the circle represents people who are in school? ____

5. What is the total number of people in the civilian labor force? _____

6. What two categories make up the civilian labor force? _____

7. **a.** Of the U.S. population over sixteen years old, what percentage is counted as

   part of the civilian labor force? ____

   b. What percentage is *not* counted as part of the civilian labor force? ____

STUDY TIP: To interpret circle graphs, look at the circle as a pie. Then try
to visualize the slices as even parts such as halves, quarters, thirds, etc.
That way you can "eyeball" (visually guess) the percentages.

Reading Charts

A chart is a way of organizing information. Charts tell you what is on television or what time the buses run. They tell you which kind of car is the best buy and how much you owe in taxes. By learning to read charts you are mastering a skill that you will use throughout your life.

To understand a chart, follow these steps:

■ Look at the *title* and read any other *headings* or explanations.

■ Look at the *pattern* or *layout.* Are there *columns*?

■ Look at the *information* described. Are there *numbers* or *symbols*? If so, what do they stand for?

■ Is there a *source* for the information?

■ Ask yourself specific *questions* about the data in the chart.

▶ The chart below shows customers' satisfaction with the cars they bought. What was the top-ranked car in this survey?

Answer: The top-ranked car was the Acura.

PRACTICE

Directions: Study the chart and answer the following questions:

1. How many drivers were surveyed? _____

2. How long had the drivers in this survey owned their cars? _____

3. What model ranked number five in customer satisfaction? _____

4. What score did the number seven car receive? _____

5. Which two cars received the same score? _____

6. Why is there no number ten car listed although the chart involves the top ten models? _____

Car Satisfaction—Top 10 Models

Ranked according to a survey of 25,200 motorists one year after buying their cars

Rank	Model	Score
1	Acura	144
2	Mercedes-Benz	138
3	Honda	135
4	Cadillac	126
5	Toyota	122
6	Lincoln	121
7	BMW	120
8	Volvo	118
9	Mazda	117
9	Audi	117

Source: J.D. Power and Associates

Challenge

If the information in this chart is accurate, what conclusion can you draw about the performance of imported cars compared to domestic cars? _____

_____

Locating Data on Charts

The chart below shows how hot the air feels at various temperatures and humidity levels.

TEMPERATURE AND HUMIDITY INDEX CHART

Air temperature in degrees Fahrenheit:

Relative Humidity	70	75	80	85	90	95	100
	Feels like:						
0%	64	69	73	78	83	87	91
10%	65	70	75	80	85	90	95
20%	66	72	77	82	87	93	99
30%	67	73	78	84	90	96	104
40%	68	74	79	86	93	101	110
50%	69	75	81	88	96	107	120
60%	70	76	82	90	100	114	132
70%	70	77	85	93	106	124	144
80%	71	78	86	97	113	136	
90%	71	79	88	102	122		
100%	72	80	91	108			

Source: 1989 World Almanac

The easiest way to learn to use a chart is to use it! What does a 90-degree temperature feel like when the humidity is 40 percent? Find the actual temperature of 90 degrees at the top of the chart. Trace your finger down that column until you are even with the 40 percent level at the side. The temperature feels like 93 degrees.

▶ How hot does it feel when the temperature is 70 degrees and the humidity is 90 percent? _____

Answer: It feels like 71°.

▶ When the temperature is 80°, but it feels like 88°, what is the humidity? _____

Answer: The humidity is 90%.

30

MORE PRACTICE

Directions: Using the Temperature and Humidity Index Chart, answer the following questions.

How hot does the air feel when the:

1. actual temperature is 80 degrees; the humidity is 50 percent? ____

2. actual temperature is 75 degrees; the humidity is 90 percent? ____

3. actual temperature is 85 degrees; the humidity is 60 percent? ____

4. actual temperature is 100 degrees; the humidity is 50 percent? ____

5. actual temperature is 70 degrees; the humidity is 100 percent? ____

How high is the relative humidity when the air temperature is:

6. 90° but feels like 100°? ____

7. 100° but feels like 104°? ____

8. 75° but feels like 80°? ____

9. 90° but feels like 106°? ____

10. 85° but feels like 78°? ____

Challenge

What does the chart show you about the relationship between humidity and temperature? The higher the humidity, the _____ the temperature feels. The lower the humidity, the _____ the temperature feels.

STUDY TIP: To interpret a chart, try to sum up in your own words the conclusion to which the information leads.

Interpreting Maps

Maps show location, direction, distance, topography or terrain, and relative size. Most maps have a **legend** or key to help you find your way. Maps also include symbols that show direction and scale.

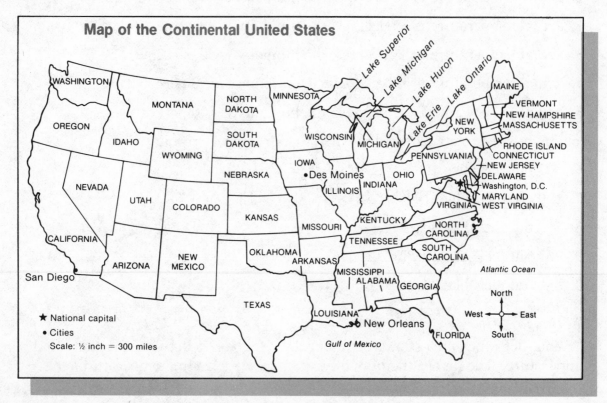

Map of the Continental United States

■ **Legend.** The legend tells what the map's symbols mean. Dots, lines, and even colors can be symbols. Blue usually represents a body of water. A star stands for a state or national capital.

■ **Direction.** On most maps, North is at the top, and South is at the bottom. East is on the right and West is on the left. An arrow or compass on the map orients you to directions, since not all maps have North at the top. Many compasses show directions in between the main ones: Northwest (NW), Northeast (NE), Southwest (SW), and Southeast (SE). Central is a direction that is not usually shown on a map. Central means located near the center or middle.

■ **Scale.** Many maps have a scale that tells you how many miles are equal to one inch on the map.

32

PRACTICE

Directions: Use the U.S. map on page 32 to answer these questions.

1. Fill in the rest of the points on this compass with the correct abbreviations.

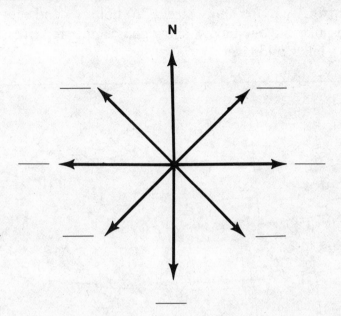

2. Name the directional locations for the following places. Use the abbreviations N, S, E, W, NE, NW, SE, SW, or write Central if it applies.

    a. San Diego, California _____

    b. Des Moines, Iowa _____

    c. New Orleans, Louisiana _____

3. What direction is Washington state from New York? _____

4. What direction is Missouri from Texas? _____

5. What direction is Arkansas from Utah? _____

6. Name the five Great Lakes in the northern United States. _____

_____

7. Approximately how many miles would *one* inch equal according to the scale on

    page 32? _____

Challenge

    Find your state on the map. Identify the city or town in which you live by using a dot like those that identify San Diego, Des Moines, and New Orleans.

More on Interpreting Maps

There are many different kinds of maps, each designed for a special purpose. Road maps show highways and roads to help us get from city to city. City maps show streets to help us find our way. Physical maps, like the one below, show geographic features, such as mountains, lakes and rivers.

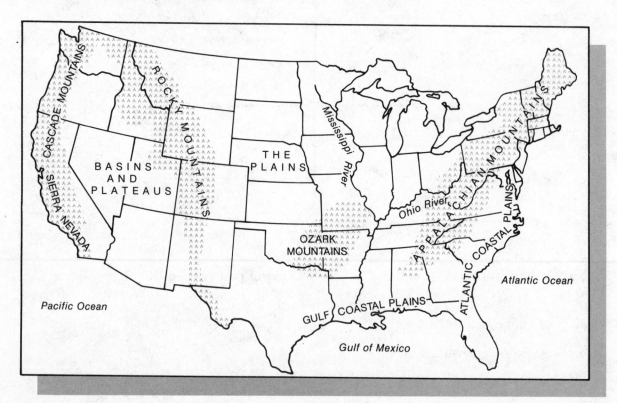

PRACTICE

Directions: Look at the map above and answer these questions.

1. What mountain range is in the eastern United States? _____

2. What waterway does the Ohio River drain into? _____

3. What type of terrain is found on much of the Pacific Coast? _____

4. What mountain range cuts through the western United States? _____

34

Reading Time Lines

Time lines show *chronology*, or the order of events or dates. You have probably made time lines yourself. As you move toward the right on a time line, you are moving forward in time. As you move toward the left on a time line, you are moving backward in time. Look at the time line below.

This time line shows significant communications discoveries. Read the date on the top and the invention written underneath it. Look at the large space between the invention of paper and the invention of movable type. That space stands for about 1,500 years. Did you notice that during the late 1800s—the time period in which the Industrial Revolution began—there were many new communications inventions?

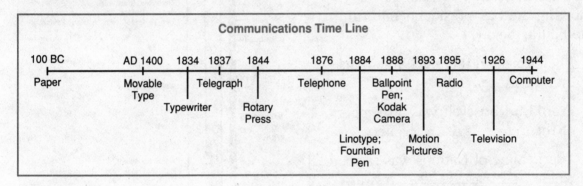

PRACTICE

Directions: Look at the communications time line and put these inventions in order from the earliest to the latest. Use 1 for the earliest and 12 for the most recent.

_____ **a.** motion pictures   _____ **g.** paper

_____ **b.** movable type   _____ **h.** telegraph

_____ **c.** television   _____ **i.** radio

_____ **d.** rotary press   _____ **j.** Kodak camera

_____ **e.** telephone   _____ **k.** computer

_____ **f.** fountain pen   _____ **l.** typewriter

Time Lines with Many Details

Here is a vertical time line that shows major historical events occurring during various U.S. presidencies. The time line tells the president and vice president at the time, and the party to which they belonged. The center line shows the spans of time in which the Democrats or Republicans were in power. The solid black line shows specific dates.

MORE PRACTICE

Directions: Study the time line showing the U.S. presidents and fill in the blanks below.

1. The circles on the black line mark every ____ years.

2. Franklin Roosevelt was a member of the _____ party.

3. The League of Nations was formed when _____ was president.

4. The San Francisco earthquake of 1906 occurred during the presidency of
_____.

5. _____ was vice president during World War I.

6. On this time line, the first president to serve two complete consecutive terms was _____.

7. This time line represents a span of how many years? _____

Do It Yourself

Make your own personal time line to show steps in a process as you move toward a certain goal. The final date represents the deadline. The dates before it are dates when certain steps must be completed.

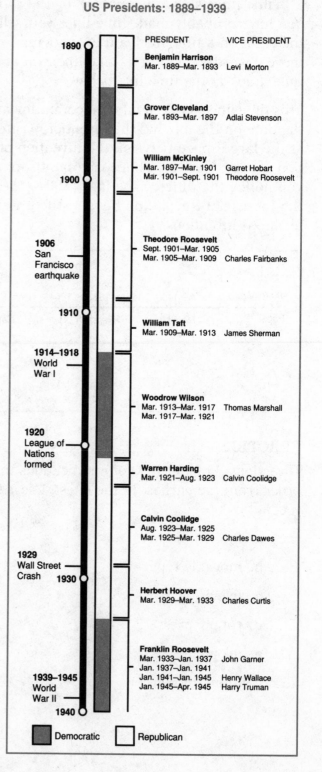

US Presidents: 1889–1939

	PRESIDENT	VICE PRESIDENT
1890	**Benjamin Harrison** Mar. 1889–Mar. 1893	Levi Morton
	Grover Cleveland Mar. 1893–Mar. 1897	Adlai Stevenson
	William McKinley Mar. 1897–Mar. 1901 Mar. 1901–Sept. 1901	Garret Hobart Theodore Roosevelt
1900		
1906 San Francisco earthquake	**Theodore Roosevelt** Sept. 1901–Mar. 1905 Mar. 1905–Mar. 1909	Charles Fairbanks
1910	**William Taft** Mar. 1909–Mar. 1913	James Sherman
1914–1918 World War I		
	Woodrow Wilson Mar. 1913–Mar. 1917 Mar. 1917–Mar. 1921	Thomas Marshall
1920 League of Nations formed		
	Warren Harding Mar. 1921–Aug. 1923	Calvin Coolidge
	Calvin Coolidge Aug. 1923–Mar. 1925 Mar. 1925–Mar. 1929	Charles Dawes
1929 Wall Street Crash 1930	**Herbert Hoover** Mar. 1929–Mar. 1933	Charles Curtis
	Franklin Roosevelt Mar. 1933–Jan. 1937 Jan. 1937–Jan. 1941 Jan. 1941–Jan. 1945 Jan. 1945–Apr. 1945	John Garner Henry Wallace Harry Truman
1939–1945 World War II 1940		

■ Democratic □ Republican

Understanding Editorial Cartoons

Editorial or political cartoons make their points through humor. Political cartoons often deal with current politics, national and world events, or economics.

Political cartoons often use these common symbols:

- A donkey is the symbol for the Democratic party.

- An elephant is the symbol for the Republican party.

- Uncle Sam symbolizes the United States.

- A bear symbolizes the Soviet Union.

A political cartoon expresses feelings or opinions by the way it portrays the characters. Asking these questions can help you to understand editorial cartoons better:

- Who are the characters and what mood do they express?

- Do they look like any famous people (for example, the president, the vice president, a senator, or a leader of another nation)?

- Is one character portrayed as being bigger or more powerful than another?

- Does one character stand for an idea or issue rather than for a real person?

To understand some cartoons, you need to understand *allusions*. Allusions often are references to figures in literature. Common allusions refer to the Bible and folk heroes. Reading editorial cartoons calls upon your knowledge of symbols, fables, and sayings you've heard over the course of most of your life.

In most cases, *captions* appear under the cartoon. Sometimes a balloon (the outline in a cartoon that encloses the words spoken or thought by the character) is included. Therefore, you need to read the words in an editorial cartoon as well as study the picture presented.

PRACTICE

Directions: Study the cartoon below and answer the questions based on it. (**Background clue:** The B-1 is an expensive bomber produced by the U.S. Air Force that is far over budget from its original projections.)

1. What is the setting for this cartoon? Where does it take place?_____

2. What does "USAF" stand for? _____

3. Is this cartoon referring to a real turkey or the slang term "turkey"? What is the meaning of "turkey" in this cartoon? _____

4. What does the egg in the coop next to the shed stand for? _____

5. What does the character mean when he says, "Call the bank, this one's eating more than we thought"? What is being eaten? _____

6. Put together all the clues and write a one-sentence explanation for the cartoon

_____

_____

MORE PRACTICE

Directions: Study the cartoon below and explain in your own words what the cartoonist is criticizing.

_____

_____

_____

_____

_____

_____

_____

STUDY TIP: One way to figure out what an editorial cartoon means is to keep abreast of current events by reading the newspaper or watching the news.

Chapter Review

Comprehension Check

Graphs and Charts

Directions: For each item below, write *chart*, *circle*, *bar*, or *line* to answer which kind of visual aid would best show the information.

_____ 1. How a federal budget was divided among programs

_____ 2. Comparison of the number of men vs. women in the armed forces in 1970, 1980, and 1990

_____ 3. The highs and lows of gasoline prices during one year

_____ 4. How the average person divides up his or her time in a twenty-four-hour day

_____ 5. Windchill factor (how wind speed affects actual air temperature)

_____ 6. The advantages and disadvantages of compact discs and audio tapes

_____ 7. A comparison of the top running speeds of ten species of animals

_____ 8. The changes over 10 years in the cost of the average automobile

Map Skills

Directions: Use the following words to complete the sentences: *compass, scale,* and *legend.*

1. The _____ tells you how many miles one inch on the map stands for.

2. The _____ shows directions on the map. North is usually at the top.

3. To find out what the map symbols stand for, look at the _____.

Time Lines

Directions: Write T for true or F for false.

_____ **1.** A time line shows directions on a map.

_____ **2.** A time line shows the order of events.

_____ **3.** A time line can show what is happening in two different places at the same time.

_____ **4.** On a time line, earlier events appear to the right of later events.

Editorial Cartoons

Directions: Match the symbol on the left with its most likely meaning on the right.

_____ **1.** turkey

_____ **2.** Uncle Sam

_____ **3.** George Washington

_____ **4.** Darth Vader

_____ **5.** donkey

_____ **6.** elephant

_____ **7.** turtle

_____ **8.** bear

_____ **9.** leaky bucket

a. United States
b. honesty, patriotism
c. Republican Party
d. loser
e. Democratic Party
f. Soviet Union
g. slowness
h. Star Wars defense system
i. U.S. budget

Reading Strategies

The strategy behind showing scenes from upcoming movies is to persuade you to see them. You can learn strategies that can help you to decide whether to read material. You can also learn strategies that help you remember more of what you read. These reading strategies are: previewing, skimming, scanning, and the SQ3R method.

By becoming familiar with these strategies, you can spend your time reading more wisely. You will be able to get the gist of a reading without having to read it word for word. You will not have to waste time reading lines of pages when you're looking for specific information only.

Words You'll Need to Know

These important words will be used in Chapter 4. Learn what each word means.

preview—to get an idea of what you will read before you read it
skim—to look quickly through a reading selection for *general* information
scan—to look quickly through a reading selection for *specific* information

---

Previewing

You already know quite a bit about **previewing**. You've learned about reading introductions, summaries, chapter headings and subheads to get an idea of the framework of a book or chapter. Previewing is a method that gives you a general idea of heavy reading materials—things that take a long time to read. Previewing helps you to determine what material is worth reading more closely. Follow these three steps to preview:

1. **Read the first one or two paragraphs of the chapter or article.** The first paragraph or two will tell you the topic and the purpose of the chapter. They usually announce to you very clearly what the chapter is about and what is important.

2. **Read the first two sentences of the middle paragraphs.** A paragraph is a unit of information. Each paragraph contains one idea. The first or second sentence of each paragraph is usually the topic sentence. It tells you the main purpose or idea of the paragraph. The rest of the paragraph contains supporting details. You can go back and read those later when you read in-depth.

3. **Read the last two paragraphs of the chapter.** The last one or two paragraphs are usually a summary of the chapter. They present in a neat package what the chapter was about and what ideas are most important to remember. Then you can keep those ideas in mind as you read the chapter in depth.

PRACTICE

Directions: Read each paragraph below. Then go back and underline the topic sentence. The topic sentence tells what the main idea of the paragraph is. In a textbook, it is usually the first or second sentence.

1. Hummingbirds are very active. They eat and burn off about 155,000 calories a day. They need all those calories because they are almost constantly in motion during the day. Their diet is mainly pure sugar from the nectar of flowers. They can fly backward, hover, fly upward like a helicopter, or turn right or left in midair. All those maneuvers take a lot of energy and a lot of wing beating. They can beat their wings from eight to eighty times in one second. They even beat their wings while they are hovering over a flower in order to feed.

2. At night hummingbirds sometimes go into a state of suspended animation called torpor. It's no wonder, since they

use so much energy during the day. During torpor, their body temperature drops to conserve energy. They don't go into this suspended state every night, though. If the food supply was scarce during the day, they go into torpor to stretch their fuel. But if feeding was good for the day, they simply sleep at night.

MORE PRACTICE

Directions: Preview the seven-paragraph article below and answer the questions that follow. Read the first and last paragraphs and the first sentence or two of each of the middle paragraphs.

1. Many people experience tooth pain at one time or another. A *toothache* is a pain in one or more teeth. It is felt as a dull throb or a sharp twinge in the affected area. By answering certain questions, you can sometimes diagnose a problem with your teeth and thereby determine how serious the problem may be.

2. The first question you should ask yourself is whether you feel the pain while biting down when eating. If you do, and if the dentist has filled your tooth within the previous week, the filling may not be level. The tooth may need further attention by the dentist. It is normal to feel twinges of pain after a filling as long as the pain does not last for more than a week.

3. On the other hand, if you feel pain after eating and the dentist has *not* filled one or more of your teeth during the previous week, you may have a cavity caused by dental decay. To relieve the pain, you will need to have the tooth filled by your dentist.

4. Sometimes you may feel pain in your tooth without biting down while eating. In this case, ask yourself whether the bouts of throbbing pain have been frequent. If the answer is *yes*, the pulp in your tooth may be inflamed because of advanced dental decay. If so, the dentist may need to perform drastic measures in order to avoid extracting the tooth. In the past, many dentists did not hesitate to pull out a severely decayed tooth. However, today most dentists will go to great lengths to preserve a patient's natural teeth.

5. If your tooth aches continuously, and if your body temperature is 100°F or above, it may be a sign that you have an *abscess*, a severe inflammation in which pus surrounds the swollen tissue. If you have symptoms that indicate an abscess, it is extremely important to consult your dentist without delay. Abscesses can lead to serious problems, spreading infection to other areas.

6. For severe toothaches, you should ask your dentist for an emergency appointment, especially if your toothache is:

- continuous
- so severe that you can't sleep
- followed by a swollen jaw or gums
- followed by a temperature of 100°F or above

7. While these tips may be helpful in helping you to decide whether to see a dentist, when in doubt always seek a professional's advice.

1. What is the topic and purpose of this reading? _____

_____

_____

2. What is the main idea of paragraph 2? _____

_____

_____

3. What is the main idea of paragraph 3? _____

_____

_____

4. What is the main idea of paragraph 5? _____

_____

_____

5. What title would you give this article? _____

_____

Now go back and read the entire article.

You should find it easy to read and comprehend because your previewing activity told you what to expect.

STUDY TIP: Preview all of your reading assignments before you read them in depth.

Skimming

Skimming is another way of getting an idea of what information is in a chapter before you actually read it. When you skim, you read quickly for general information and main ideas. You skim a reading selection to:

- get a bird's-eye view of what it's about

- get general information

- find new information when you're familiar with the topic

Here's how you skim. Sweep the page visually for key words and topics. Pick up only a few key words in each line. You'll find that important words and concepts jump out at you!

Look at the following passage from a book on parenting. Imagine you just want to get a general idea of what the passage is saying, so you decide to skim it. You quickly read the opening sentence and then look for key words that give important information. To help get you used to the idea of skimming, the opening sentence and key words have been printed in **dark** type. Simply read these words and then answer the question below.

> **Sometimes problems that are not directly related to your baby can interfere with your care of the baby.** If you realize that you are not caring properly for your infant, it's possible that a **family problem** is to **blame**. Perhaps you are having difficulties with **another child** in the family or with your **husband or wife**. If you are not having problems with your family, you might want to **look at other aspects of your life: problems** you might be having with **other relatives** or with **friends**, **financial** concerns, problems at **work**, **illnesses**, and so on. You may find a long list of difficulties that are distracting you from your baby.

Question: What problems can interfere with a parent's care of his or her baby? _____

_____

_____

In your answer, you should have noted that problems with other family members, relatives or friends, financial matters, work, and health can all distract a parent from an infant.

PRACTICE

Directions: Skim this article about maple sugaring. It should take you less than a minute to skim it. Then, underline the main idea of each paragraph and circle the key words that "jump out" at you. The first paragraph is done as an example.

Maple Sugaring

Maple sugar time means springtime in New England. Sugaring begins with the first thaw in March. The days have to be warm and the nights freezing for the sap to rise in the tree and drip into the buckets.

Native Americans taught the early New England settlers how to extract the sweet sap from the maple trees and boil it down to a sugary syrup. According to one legend, when the world was first created, syrup itself flowed from the trees. But the Great Spirit decided that people ought to have to work harder for something so delicious and sweet.

Maple sugar farmers tap the trees by drilling a hole and inserting a spout called a tap. Traditional sugarers hang buckets from the taps to collect the sap. The buckets of sap are brought into a sugar shack to be boiled down into syrup.

The sap is boiled in a huge pot over a wood fire. The sap from the tree is as thin as water. It takes about forty gallons of sap to make one gallon of syrup. It takes a lot of wood to keep that fire going too.

Modern syrup producers have replaced the buckets with plastic tubing. The tubes run directly from the tree tap to the sugar shack. The wood fires have been replaced with modern stoves and furnaces.

STUDY TIP: When you are skimming, lightly underline words that jump out at you. Those words often turn out to be part of the main idea.

Scanning

You use **scanning** often. You scan when you look for a name in a phone book or look up a word in a dictionary or glossary. You scan when you look in the paper for your favorite baseball team's standing.

Scanning is another quick way of reading. But it has the opposite purpose of skimming. When you skim, you are reading for general information. When you scan, you are reading for *specific* information. Here's how to scan:

■ Let your eyes glide across the page.

■ Repeat in your mind the key information you are looking for—a date, a place name, a person's name, keys such as quotation marks, italics, etc.

■ When looking for a person or place name, focus on words with capital letters. If you are looking for a date, or amount, focus on numbers.

■ Move your eyes quickly across the page looking for key words, capital letters or numbers. When you scan, the words you are looking for will pop out at you.

PRACTICE

Directions: Scan each paragraph below for the information asked for. Keep key words and clues in your mind as your eyes sweep the paragraph for the answer. Write down the keys you will look for as you scan. Then scan the paragraph. It should take you several seconds. Then write the answer to the question in the space below the paragraph. The first one is started for you.

1. In what countries do tree shrews live?

Keys: names of countries, words with capital letters

The common tree shrew has little hair. It looks like a squirrel with a long snout. These small animals are constantly on the move as they look for food in trees and on the ground. Their diet consists mostly of insects, but they also feed on fruit, seeds, and leaves. They live in forests in parts of Nepal, China, Sumatra, and Java.

Answer: *Nepal*, _____, _____, _____

2. How many films did Charlie Chaplin make?

Keys: _____

      Charlie Chaplin was a comic genius. His most famous character was the Little Tramp, known for his baggy pants, bowler hat, and floppy shoes. He was at the height of his popularity during the 1920s in the era of silent films. He continued to make silent films into the 1940s, when most of the film industry was making "talkies." Between 1914 and 1967, he made 81 feature and short films. His first film was *Making a Living* in 1914. It was 53 years later that he made *A Countess from Hong Kong*.

Answer: _____

3. What does the word *robot* mean?

Keys: _____

      Robots were "invented" by a Czech writer, Karel Capek. In 1921, he wrote a play called *R.U.R.*, which stands for "Rossum's Universal Robot." In Czech, *robot* means "worker" or "forced laborer." In the play, Rossum created beings that looked human but were actually mechanical. They were artificial human beings. Robots today are computerized machines that are capable of doing many tasks, especially on factory production lines.

Answer: _____

Challenge

1. If you are reading the want ads and looking for a job as a waiter, do you think you will skim or scan the ads? _____

Why? _____

2. If you are reading the want ads for any job at all, will you skim or scan the ads? _____

Why? _____

STUDY TIP: When you scan, repeat in your mind the key word or clue you are looking for. The answers will pop out from the text.

Following the SQ3R Method

SQ3R is a strategy for studying. It stands for:

S	Survey
Q	Question
R	Read
R	Recite
R	Review

The best way to learn this way of studying is to do it! To do the rest of this lesson, choose a chapter or part of a chapter in one of your textbooks. Or get a book or article about a subject that interests you.

■ **Step 1: Survey.** You already know about the first step—*survey.* You have learned about reading chapter heads, introductions, summaries, and study questions before studying a chapter. You have also learned about previewing and skimming. They are methods of surveying. Now survey your reading selection. Which method will you use?

■ **Step 2: Question.** The next step is *question.* Read with a purpose. Look for the answers to specific questions as you read. If there are headings, turn them into questions and then read to find the answers. For example, if you turned the title *The Rights of Consumers* into a question, it would read: *What are the rights of consumers?*

▶ Turn to the reading selection you chose. If your reading selection has headings, turn them into questions. Write the questions here.

1. _____

2. _____

3. _____

4. _____

5. _____

■ **Step 3: Read.** Now *read* the text carefully. Spend time studying any illustrations and graphs. Be sure that you have found the answers to your questions before moving on to the next section.

■ **Step 4: Recite.** After you read each section, *recite* the answers to your questions. Reciting what you have read helps reinforce the information. You can take notes as a form of reciting. We will look at note taking in the next lesson.

▶ Now recite the main points you read in your selection.

■ **Step 5: Review.** When you are done reciting, *review* what you have read. Do it right away so that you will remember more. Studying for tests will be easier if you review right away. Once again, look at the chapter introduction and summary, any study questions, headings or main points in the section, and any notes you took.

▶ Review your reading selection now. Answer the questions you wrote in Step 2 on the blanks below.

1. _____

_____

2. _____

_____

3. _____

_____

4. _____

_____

5. _____

_____

PRACTICE

Directions: Turn each of these subheads into a question that starts with *Who, What, Where, When, Why,* or *How.* Be sure that your question requires more than a yes-no answer.

1. The Influence of the Iroquois Confederacy on the U.S. Constitution

_____

2. The Television Signal—from the Station to Your Home

_____

3. The Greatest Leader of the Twentieth Century

_____

Note Taking

Activity reinforces learning. By taking notes on your reading, you are helping to remember the information. You are storing it in your mind so that you can retrieve it later.

Note taking can be part of the SQ3R study method. You can take notes instead of *reciting* the information in each section.

Here are a few tips for taking good study notes from your textbooks:

- **Keep all your notes for each subject together.** Keep them in a notebook.

- **Keep your notes brief.** You don't have to use complete sentences. Try to take only one page of notes for each chapter. You are taking notes to help jog your memory when you study them later on.

- **Use headings.** Use the headings in the text as your headings— or use the questions you turned them into. Underline those headings or questions. Then write the answers or main points underneath your headings.

- **Write down key words and terms and a definition for each.**

- **Write page numbers in parentheses.** In this way, you can easily find the information again in your textbook.

PRACTICE

Directions: Here's a way of setting up notes using an outline. Make notes for the reading selection you worked with in the previous lesson on SQ3R.

Name of chapter or article: _____

I. First heading written as a question: _____

    A. Important information: _____

_____

    B. Key words and definitions: _____

_____

II. Next heading written as a question: _____

    A. Important information: _____

_____

    B. Key words and definitions: _____

_____

To save space and time when you are taking notes, you can shorten words, as long as you know what the abbreviations mean. Here are some examples:

gov't.	government	*w/*	with
hist.	history	*sim.*	similarities
=	is (or means)	*dif.*	differences
@	at	*aft.*	after

Sometimes it's useful to use lists in your notes. Suppose the name of your chapter is "U.S. Economy vs. Soviet Economy." The abbreviation *vs.* tells you that the two economic systems are going to be compared and contrasted. You might want to set up a simple list:

U.S.S.R.
Gov't. control of production

U.S.
Private ownership

If you had several categories, your list might become a chart. Here's another way of setting up a list about the Soviet economy and the American economy.

	U.S.S.R.	*U.S.*
Ownership	Gov't. ownershp.	Pvt. ownershp.
Social programs	Gov't. provides housing, health care, educ.	Gov't. and pvt.
Economic freedom	Limited choices of jobs, goods	Free choice, open mkt.

MORE PRACTICE

Directions: Write your own abbreviations for these words:

International _____   senator _____
between _____   definition _____
Czechoslovakia _____   trigonometry _____
president _____   governor _____
vice president _____   department _____
biology _____   tablespoon _____
psychology _____   superintendent _____
vitamins _____   calorie _____

STUDY TIP: To better remember information, write the information in your own words.

Drawing Thought Webs

Our thoughts do not usually move from point to point as an outline does. We have one thought and that thought leads to another. We make connections and associations among ideas.

A weblike style of note taking is based on the way our minds work. It is visual. We can see connections. The web allows us to see a big picture of the idea being discussed. Thought webs or branches can be useful when

- taking notes during a lecture

- planning a written report

- reviewing information before a test

The example below shows a thought web concerning pollution.

When you make a thought web, you write the topic in a circle at the center of the page. The main ideas or questions flow directly from the circle. Details, results, and less important information branch off from those ideas toward the outside of the web. You can have as many levels or branches as you need.

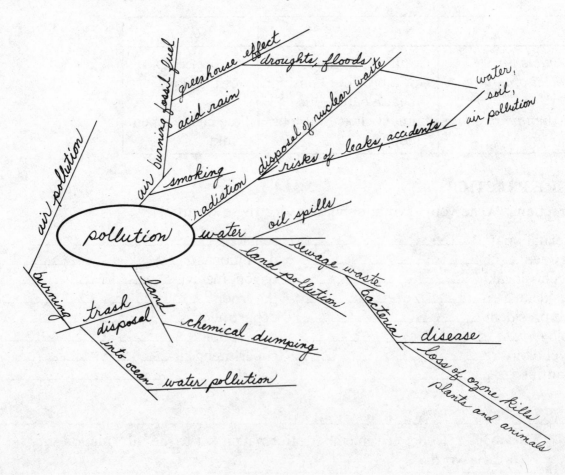

PRACTICE

Directions: Refer to the web on page 54 to answer the questions.

1. What is the topic of this web? _____

2. What are the four main topics coming from the center?

   _____

3. Name two effects of burning fossil fuels.

   _____

4. Name two forms of land pollution.

   _____

5. Name two problems of radiation pollution.

   _____

With the web method, there is room to easily add new information. You can *see* connections and patterns. You will be able to make your own connections. Every thought web will have a different pattern.

MORE PRACTICE

Directions: Read the paragraph below. On another sheet of paper draw your own thought web for it.

Photosynthesis is a process by which plants make food. Plants use sunlight and the chlorophyll in their leaves to convert water and carbon dioxide into sugar and oxygen. Photosynthesis involves several steps. In step one, the plant absorbs light through its leaves. In step two, the plant uses the energy it gets from the sunlight to split water into oxygen and hydrogen. In step three, the oxygen is released into the atmosphere and the hydrogen combines with carbon dioxide to produce sugar.

STUDY TIP: Your notes are for your personal use when you study and review. Use whatever method or combination of methods helps you to learn and remember.

Using Memory Aids

Writing notes helps you to remember. Saying the information out loud helps too. But there are many other ways to remember. Some people remember by seeing the information. Others remember by associating the information with jingles or by hearing the information. Here are some techniques for you to try:

■ **Repetition.** If you **repeat** information often enough and use it, you will remember it. Even people who claim to have poor memories usually can remember phone numbers that they call often.

■ **Chunking.** One way of remembering numbers and letters is by **chunking**, or putting groups of words, letters, or numbers together. You see them at once in your mind: 555-3271, UFO, NAACP. To remember lists of words, you can chunk. For example, you can remember a list of nations by breaking it into two groups of three with an organizing label. The organizing labels for the groups of countries below are *North America* and *Eastern Europe*:

United States, Canada, Mexico	Soviet Union, Poland, Romania

■ **Catch words and sentences.** Some strings of letters are easy to learn. For example, the spaces on a treble clef scale in music spell out *FACE.* But what about the letters of the lines— EGBDF? Musicians teach their students a phrase to remember: "*Every Good Boy Deserves Fudge.*"

If there is a list of words to remember, you can take the first letter of each word and make up a nonsense word or sentence that you will remember. The first letter from each word in the list will jog your memory.

To remember the primary colors you might remember the word *ruby* which stands for "*r*ed, *b*lue, *y*ellow." Or if you remember by seeing, you might picture a rainbow with those three colors.

■ **Rhymes and verses.** How do you remember the number of days in each month? A common verse that contains this information is: "Thirty days hath September, April, June, and November; all the rest have thirty-one, except February, which has twenty-eight and in leap year twenty-nine."

■ **Flash Cards.** As you learned before, writing down information helps you remember it. Flash cards can help you remember dates of events, definitions for foreign words, or key words relating to a particular subject. The action of turning the card over and seeing the answer imprints the information on your memory. You can also post notes or cards where you can see them often.

PRACTICE

1. How would you remember the names of the planets in our solar system? Make up a sentence or saying to remember their names, or chunk them in order to remember.

   Mercury, Venus, Earth, Mars, Jupiter, Saturn, Uranus, Neptune, Pluto.

   Write your memory aid here: _____

   _____

   _____

2. How would you remember the names of the continents? Make up a catch word or sentence to remember their names.

   Africa, Antarctica, Asia, Australia, Europe, North America, South America.

   Write your catch word or sentence here: _____

   _____

   _____

3. How would you remember the names of the original 13 colonies? Chunk them in order to remember.

   New York, Rhode Island, Massachusetts, Connecticut, New Jersey, Delaware, Pennsylvania, Virginia, North Carolina, South Carolina, Maryland, Georgia, New Hampshire.

   _____

   _____

STUDY TIP: Make flash cards for unfamiliar terms in a subject you are studying. Have someone test your knowledge of the terms.

Improving Listening Skills

The notes that you take are only as good as the information you are able to pick up. Here are some tips that can help you improve your listening skill.

- **Keep an open mind.** By having an open mind, you will be receptive toward the subject and the teacher. A closed mind shuts down the listening process.

- **Use your eyes and ears.** A speaker gives clues about what he or she thinks is important. Even the most boring speaker gives some clues with gestures, tone of voice, and volume.

- **Read the assignment before class.** If you are already somewhat familiar with the material, you will be able to understand the teacher better and take part in a discussion.

- **Listen for summaries of what was just said.** Listen for transition sentences that tell you the teacher is making a new point; for example, "*Now* we'll talk about . . ." "We just talked about . . ." Listen for words that emphasize, such as "Remember" and "It's important to know . . ."

- **Ask questions if you don't understand something.**

- **Answer questions.** Take part in class discussions. Listen to what other students have to say too. The more you participate, the more alert you will be.

- **Take notes as you listen.** Note what your teacher emphasizes. What does he or she ask questions about? The teacher is giving you clues about what he or she thinks is important. Pay special attention to those points, especially when you are reviewing for the next class or for a test.

The following exercise can help you improve your listening skills. With practice, you can become a great listener.

Break up into pairs. You will take turns being the speaker and the listener. The speaker can choose any topic he or she can speak about for three to five minutes.

1. The listener listens without saying a word. When the time is up, the listener summarizes what the speaker said.

2. When you are the listener, don't form any judgments or opinions. Simply restate, in your own words, what the speaker said. Your summary should be about thirty to forty-five seconds. Tell what the topic was and what the main points were.

Chapter Review

Successful Student Checklist

Here are some things that can help you win at studying. Put a check ☑ in the box of each one that you do.

☐ You get an idea of what you will read by previewing the material.

☐ You get a general idea of information in a chapter by skimming.

☐ You scan reading material to quickly find specific information.

☐ You use the SQ3R strategy to study material on which you will be tested.

☐ You take notes to help you remember information.

☐ You use abbreviations to save space and time when taking notes.

☐ You use memory aids to help you remember.

☐ You listen actively so that you can take good notes.

Comprehension Check

Previewing

Directions: Write T for true or F for false next to each statement.

_____ **1.** Previewing is a way to remember the material contained in a chapter.

_____ **2.** When previewing, you should always read every paragraph carefully.

_____ **3.** The first two paragraphs of a chapter often tell the topic and purpose of the chapter.

_____ **4.** Chapter headings and subheads give you an idea of the structure of the chapter.

_____ **5.** The topic sentence of a paragraph usually tells the main idea of the paragraph.

Skimming and Scanning

Directions: For each item below, write *skim* or *scan* according to which method you would use for the reading material.

_____ **1.** To find out the date of the first battle of the Civil War

_____ **2.** To get an idea of what's in the chapter

_____ **3.** To read information with which you are already familiar

_____ **4.** To look for a specific answer to a question

_____ **5.** To look for general information

_____ **6.** To look up a phone number

SQ3R

Directions: Write the five steps to SQ3R:

S _____ R _____

Q _____ R _____

R _____

Note Taking

Directions: Circle the letter of the answer that best completes each sentence.

1. Note taking can be part of the SQ3R method. It can be done instead of
   a. surveying
   b. reciting
   c. questioning

2. To best remember the information,
   a. put it into your own words
   b. copy it word for word from the book
   c. use a loose-leaf notebook

3. Lists are handy for
   a. comparing and contrasting
   b. remembering where to find the information
   c. sorting out abbreviations

4. The main purpose of note taking is to
   a. remind you of the chapter headings
   b. help you learn abbreviations
   c. help you remember the main points

Memory Aids

Directions: Name three memory aids.

_____ _____ _____

Listening

Directions: Put a check mark next to each item that is a good active listening habit.

_____ 1. Taking notes

_____ 2. Listening to tone of voice

_____ 3. Doing stretching exercises during a class discussion

_____ 4. Writing down every word the teacher says

_____ 5. Asking questions

Chapter 5
Using Reference Tools

Many resources are available for you to use in carrying out and completing your classroom assignments. These resources are tools that you can use to help succeed in your school work. They come in the form of dictionaries, atlases, and other types of references. Each time you use one of these resources, your skill and speed in finding the needed information will improve.

Words You'll Need to Know

These important words will be used in Chapter 5. Read what each word means.

alphabetize—to put words in A-B-C order

etymology—an explanation of where a word came from originally

thesaurus—a book containing listings of synonyms (words that are similar in meaning)

reference books—books consulted for the specific information they provide

periodical—a magazine

Putting Words in Alphabetical Order

If you have ever used a phone book to look up a number, then you already know about **alphabetizing**. This lesson will give you some practice finding information more quickly.

It's clear enough how to alphabetize words if all the words begin with different letters like those below:

| animal | ferment | jade | kangaroo | timber | x-ray |

But what if the words begin with the same letter or letters? Then you must compare the second, third, or even fourth or fifth letters until you find the letter that is different. Then decide which of those letters comes first in the alphabet.

Look at these two words: **savior—savor**

The first three letters are the same—*s-a-v*, but the fourth letters are different: sav*i*or, sav*o*r

▶ Which word would be listed first in an alphabetical listing? Look at the fourth letter: *i* comes before *o*, so *savior* is listed first.

▶ What if you run out of letters *before* you find a letter that is different? For example: **but—butt**

Then the shorter word is listed first—*but, butt*.

PRACTICE

Directions: List these words in alphabetical order:

| synonym relativity planetarium pontiff receptacle synthesis |
| rhinoceros plate symmetry symphony posthumous pleasant |

1. _____   7. _____

2. _____   8. _____

3. _____   9. _____

4. _____   10. _____

5. _____   11. _____

6. _____   12. _____

MORE PRACTICE

Directions: Alphabetize each set of three words.

1. China, chimpanzee, chrome

   _____

   _____

   _____

2. hummingbird, humming, humiliation

   _____

   _____

   _____

3. divination, dividend, diversity

   _____

   _____

   _____

4. iniquity, inhumane, initiate

   _____

   _____

   _____

5. electromagnetic, electroscope, electrode

   _____

   _____

   _____

6. junta, juniper, junior

   _____

   _____

   _____

7. abacus, abate, abashed

   _____

   _____

   _____

8. sensible, sensuous, sensation

   _____

   _____

   _____

9. gadfly, gadabout, gadget

   _____

   _____

   _____

10. quarrel, quarter, quarry

   _____

   _____

   _____

STUDY TIP: To alphabetize words that have the same beginning letters, compare the second letters of each word. Then alphabetize by starting with the letter that comes first alphabetically.

Using Guide Words in the Dictionary

To find a word in the dictionary, look at the **guide words** at the top of each page. The purpose of guide words is to help you find the word you're seeking. Words beginning with the same two letters are alphabetized according to the third letter, words beginning with the same three letters are alphabetized by the fourth letter, and so on.

▶ Look at the guide words from three pages below. On what page would you find the word *success*? What are the guide words for that page?

348	Swahili		swashing
346	subterfuge		succinct
344	stumpage		style

Answer: page _____ guide words _____

The word *success* comes between *subterfuge* and *succinct* (*e* comes before *i*):

SUBterfuge   SUCCEss   SUCCInct

You may have to look at several letters in a word before you can decide what dictionary page it falls on.

PRACTICE

Directions: The two guide words for the page on which the words below appear are *mineral* and *minks*. Put these words in alphabetical order: ministry, miniscule, miniseries, ministate, miniskirt, minister, ministrant, ministration.

1. _____   5. _____

2. _____   6. _____

3. _____   7. _____

4. _____   8. _____

MORE PRACTICE

Directions: For each word below, decide whether it would appear between the listed guide words. If it does, write *yes*. If not, write *ahead* or *back* according to where in the dictionary you would go to find the correct page for the given word. An example is done for you.

consume   contact/contentious   *back*

1. house   hour/House of Lords   _____*yes*_____
2. tropic   triturator/troll   _____
3. temper   teach/technetium   _____
4. beggar   beggar's lice/beige   _____
5. horoscope   hornworm/horse mackerel   _____
6. lieutenant   life/light   _____
7. douse   doubletalk/down   _____
8. cartoon   carriage/carton   _____
9. apple   apostrophe/appetite   _____
10. heredity   herd/hero   _____
11. zenith   zero/zizith   _____
12. voice   volume/voted   _____
13. yeast   yearner/yesteryear   _____
14. electric   electrician/electronics   _____
15. farmhouse   farm/fashion   _____
16. riffraff   rick/riffling   _____
17. wassail   warthog/waste   _____
18. ooze   opine/optical art   _____
19. gnu   gnawer/goaltender   _____
20. innuendo   ingrain/initiation   _____

Improving Spelling and Hyphenation

Use a dictionary to look up the correct spelling or hyphenation of a word. How do you look up a word when you don't know how to spell it? Sometimes you just have to guess at the spelling in order to look it up. Is it *w-e-i-r-d* or *w-i-e-r-d*? Look under both spellings. Sound out the word. If you aren't sure, guess. If you're not right, try another way of spelling it.

PRACTICE

Directions: In the list that follows, decide if a word is spelled correctly. If it is, write *OK*. If it is not spelled correctly, rewrite the word with the correct spelling. Use your dictionary to help you.

1. labratory _____

2. anonymous _____

3. consensus _____

4. diptheria _____

5. bookeeper _____

6. Febuary _____

7. harrass _____

8. mischievous _____

9. mispell _____

Hyphenation

When you write or type a paper, you may have to divide a word at the end of a line. The dictionary tells you how to divide the word into syllables. When you divide a word you *hyphenate*, or separate syllables with a hyphen (-).

In most dictionaries, a dot divides the word into syllables. Look at the example below:

bob•cat

The dot divides *bobcat* into two syllables: *bob* and *cat*.

► How many syllables are there in the word *com•mu•ni•ca•tion*?

Write the number of syllables here. ____

If you need to divide the word at the end of the first syllable, you would write *com-* at the end of the line and *munication* on the next line.

The dictionary also tells you whether to spell a word with a hyphen. When you see a hyphen in an entry word, that hyphen is part of the spelling of that word:

deep-sea

There is a hyphen in the entry word. That means you would keep the hyphen in the word *deep-sea*. If you find the word *clean-cut* in the dictionary, how would you write the word in your paper?

You may have to look in a dictionary to find out whether a term is two separate words or a hyphenated word. Is this entry one word or two: *sea shore*? Some words are hyphenated or not depending on the role they play in a sentence.

The dictionary also tells you whether a word should begin with a capital letter. For example, this entry is two separate words. The first one begins with a capital letter:

May fly

MORE PRACTICE

Directions: Look at each of these dictionary entries. Write the number of syllables in each word. Then write each word as you would write it without showing syllables. The first one is done for you.

1. self-cen•tered   3   self-centered

2. deer•skin   —   _____

3. deep-dish pie   —   _____

4. op•ti•mis•tic   —   _____

5. hob•by•horse   —   _____

6. Dix•ie•land   —   _____

7. be•liev•ing   —   _____

Challenge

Use your dictionary to divide these words into syllables:

1. marshmallow _____

2. technologically _____

3. xylophone _____

> **STUDY TIP:** When looking for a word's correct spelling or hyphenation, focus on the entry word in bold type. Look for dots, hyphens, or spaces between syllables.

Looking Up Word Meanings

A word can have many meanings. Moreover, a word can be used as several different parts of speech. The parts of speech are noun, verb, adjective, adverb, preposition, conjunction, and interjection. The dictionary tells you the word's meaning and what part of speech it is. Abbreviations also tell you whether a word is singular or plural.

PRACTICE

Directions: Write what each of these abbreviations stands for. All of them were mentioned in the paragraph above.

1. conj. _____

2. pl. _____

3. v. _____

4. adj. _____

5. sing. _____

6. adv. _____

7. n. _____

8. prep. _____

How Dictionaries Are Organized

Dictionaries differ in the way that they list meanings. *Webster's New World Dictionary* and *Webster's New Collegiate Dictionary* list word meanings in the order of their historical development, from the earliest to the most recent. Other dictionaries, however, may arrange definitions according to usage, with the most common meaning listed first. The *American Heritage Dictionary* lists the central meaning first. That is the meaning from which the other meanings flow.

In the front of every dictionary, there is a section generally called "A Guide to the Dictionary." Look in that front section under "Arrangement of Entries" or "Definitions" to find out how meanings are listed in your dictionary.

Here's how the word *taper* appears in *Webster's New World Dictionary*:

> **tap·er** (taʹper) **n.** [ME < OE *tapur*, prob. by dissimilation < *papyrus* (see *paper*): from use of papyrus pith as wick] **1** a wax candle, esp. a long, slender one **2** a long wick coated with wax, used for lighting candles, lamps, etc. **3** any feeble light. **4** *a)* a gradual decrease in width or thickness [the *taper* of a pyramid] *b)* a gradual decrease in action, power, etc. **5** something that tapers—**adj.** gradually decreased in breadth or thickness toward one end—**vt.,** **vi. 1** to decrease gradually in width or thickness **2** to lessen; diminish—**taper off 1** to become smaller gradually toward one end **2** to diminish or stop gradually

The first five definitions tell about *taper* as a noun (**n.**). *Taper* can also be an adjective (**adj.**) or a verb (**v.**, **vt.**, or **vi.**).

When you see an unfamiliar word in a sentence, first try to determine what role it plays in the sentence. When you look the word up in the dictionary, be sure to look for noun definitions if the word is a noun, verb definitions if it's a verb, and so on. You may still have to skim through several definitions to find the right one for the sentence.

▶ Write the definition that applies to *taper* in this sentence: The doctor said Carlos's use of the crutches would *taper* off as his leg healed.

Answer: to lessen; diminish (verb)

The exact form of the word you are looking up may not be an entry word in the dictionary. For example, the past tense of *taper* is *tapered*. To find *tapered*, look up *taper*.

PRACTICE

Directions: For each word below, write the word you would look up to find the definition.

1. pampered _____

2. gripped _____

3. tried _____

4. lovingly _____

5. wrung _____

6. wrote _____

7. women _____

8. restored _____

9. bought _____

10. agreeable _____

MORE PRACTICE

Directions: Use a dictionary to find the definition of the underlined word in each sentence below. Write the part of speech (noun, verb, etc.) and the definition that applies.

1. John was so <u>vain</u> that he spent hours getting dressed every morning.

_____

_____

2. Lois <u>exhausted</u> her savings account to keep her car running.

_____

_____

3. Throughout the entire trial, he <u>maintained</u> he was innocent.

_____

_____

4. Dr. Smithers took <u>umbrage</u> at Janet's remark. _____

_____

5. Penny's insulting remark <u>reduced</u> Mary to tears. _____

_____

6. Delores fastened the <u>frogs</u> on her custom-made jacket.

_____

_____

7. The <u>overhead</u> for running the secretarial service was more than Beryl had anticipated.

_____

_____

8. Upon Glenn's arrival at La Guardia Airport, the customs official asked him if he had anything to <u>declare</u>.

_____

_____

> **S**TUDY TIP: When you look up a word, use your skimming skills to find the meaning that applies to the specific reading context. Then read the appropriate definition carefully.

Using Pronunciation Keys

Pronunciation is another kind of information the dictionary provides. The pronunciation is shown in parentheses next to the entry. The spelling in the parentheses is a guide for pronouncing the word.

hap•py (hap′ē)

In the guide at the front of the dictionary, you will find an explanation of the markings used in the pronunciations. You will also find a shorter key to the markings at the bottoms of the dictionary pages.

■ A bar (–) over a vowel stands for a long sound. The vowel is pronounced just as you would say the name of the letter; for example: ā sounds like the *a* in *pay, late,* or *fate.*

■ An upside-down arc (◡) over a vowel means the vowel has a short sound, as in *pet, pit, pat,* or *pot.*

■ Look at the accent mark (′) after the first syllable of *happy.* That mark tells you that the first syllable gets more emphasis when you say it: **hap**py.

■ In words of three syllables or more, there may be two accent marks. The **bolder** (darker) accent mark tells you which syllable gets the most emphasis. The other accent mark tells you which syllable is second in emphasis.

sat•is•fy (săt′ĭs-fī′)

You would pronounce *satisfy*: **sat**isfy.

PRACTICE

Directions: For this first group of words, say the word to yourself, then circle the syllable that gets the most emphasis. The first one is done for you.

1. sardine   sar (dine)

2. planet   plan et

3. federal   fed er al

4. ultimate   ul ti mate

5. example   ex am ple

6. distribute   dis trib ute

Here is a list of dictionary pronunciations. Look at the pronunciation guide in parentheses. Then in the word on the left, circle the syllable that the dictionary puts the stress on. The first one is done for you.

7. maple (mā′pl)

8. antithesis (ăn-tĭth′e-sĭs)

9. nuclear (nōō′klē-er)

10. motivate (mō′te-vāt′)

11. cellophane (sel′e-fān′)

12. elevation (el-e-vā′shen)

71

Looking Up Word Origins

The dictionary is a treasure chest of information. The **etymology** (word origin) is given in brackets after the pronunciation or after the list of definitions. The etymology traces the development of the word to its present meaning. Understanding the original meaning may help you remember the word's present meaning.

Here are some abbreviations and their meanings that are used in the dictionary to show etymology:

L.	Latin	O Fr.	Old French
Gr.	Greek	It.	Italian
G.	German	ME.	Middle English
Fr.	French	Heb.	Hebrew
<	derived from		

Words may have developed from other languages, or they may be combinations of two English words.

A *dormitory* is a room or building that provides sleeping quarters. Where did that word come from? Here's what the *Webster's New World Dictionary* says:

[*L.dormitorium*, place for sleeping < *dormitorius*, of or for sleeping < *dormire* to sleep]

▶ What Latin word was *dormitory* originally derived from? _____

Answer: *dormitorium*

PRACTICE

Directions: Use your own dictionary to find the origins of the words below. Write down the language, the earliest foreign word the English word can be traced to, and the meaning of the foreign word. (Keep following the "derived from" symbol (<) to the last word.)

1. fun _____

_____

2. multiple _____

_____

3. insomnia _____

_____

4. adhere _____

_____

Choosing Words in a Thesaurus

A **thesaurus** is a book of listings of synonyms. The word *thesaurus* means "treasury of words." Synonyms are words that have the same—or almost the same—meaning. The most famous thesaurus is *Roget's Thesaurus*.

A thesaurus is very handy when you are writing a paper. It can help you find just the right word to express yourself precisely. Words are arranged in a thesaurus in two ways—dictionary entry and index entry.

Dictionary Entry Thesaurus

In a thesaurus with a *dictionary entry,* the entries are arranged alphabetically. Look up words as you would in a dictionary. This kind of thesaurus is often called a *college* or *collegiate* thesaurus.

The following is from *Roget's College Thesaurus*:

> **trust**, n. & v.—n. faith, reliance, confidence, credence, BELIEF; hope, expectation, anticipation; office, charge, task, duty, custody, keeping; CREDIT; cartel, monopoly, association.—v. rely, depend, count; commit, entrust, consign, believe, hope, expect; commission; give credit to. See SAFETY. Ant., see DOUBT

What do the words in all capital letters mean? They indicate that if you look up the capitalized word, under its own entry, you will find other synonyms for trust.

What does *Ant.* stand for? It is the abbreviation for *antonym.* An antonym is a word that means the opposite of the listed word.

The opposite of *trust* is *doubt.* To find a complete listing of other antonyms for *trust,* look up the entry for *doubt.*

▶ Write the first two verb synonyms for *trust.* _____

Answer: rely; depend

▶ Under what entries would you find other synonyms for the noun form of *trust*?

_____ and _____

Answer: BELIEF; CREDIT

PRACTICE

Directions: Use these entries from *Roget's College Thesaurus* to answer the questions below.

> **vie**, v. rival, emulate; contend, strive, compete. See CONTENTION.
> **view**, n. & v.—n. sight; panorama, vista, prospect, scene; viewpoint, angle; opinion, BELIEF, notion; APPEARANCE, aspect.—v. see; survey, scan; watch, witness; consider, regard, study. See VISION, THOUGHT.
> **vigilance**, CARE; guardedness, watchfulness, alertness; wide-awakeness; caution. *Ant.*, see NEGLECT.

1. List three synonyms for *vie*. _____

2. Write two other entries under which to look up synonyms for *view* as a noun.

_____   _____

3. Write a word that means the opposite of *vigilance*. _____

Directions: Use the thesaurus entry above to choose the word you think is best to use in place of the underlined word in each sentence.

4. The two tennis pros have <u>vied</u> with each other for this championship title five

times before. _____

5. The <u>view</u> from the rim of the canyon was breathtaking. _____

Index Entry Thesaurus

If you have a thesaurus with an *index entry,* look up the word in the back of the thesaurus first. You will find an entry number there.

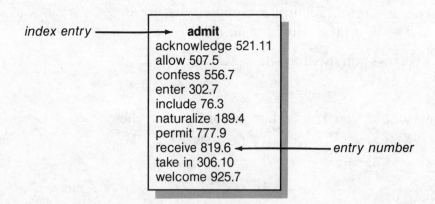

(adapted from *Roget's International Thesaurus*, fourth edition)

As you can see, the word *admit* has many shades of meaning. Choose the entry closest to the meaning you want. Then find the numbered entry in the thesaurus.

▶ Which entry would you look up for a synonym for *admit* in the following sentence?

Clark *admitted* that he had stolen the car. _____

Answer: The word closest in meaning is *confess*. Under the entry 556 in the thesaurus, you would look for paragraph 7. In entry 556.7, you would find a paragraph of synonyms for *admit*.

MORE PRACTICE

Directions: For each sentence below, decide which entry in the thesaurus would probably list the synonym you wanted for *appreciate*. Write the word and entry number on the blank line after each sentence. Then rewrite the sentence using the word or words closest in meaning to the synonym.

> **appreciate**
> be grateful 949.3
> enjoy 865.10
> increase 38.6
> know 475.12
> respect 964.4
> understand 548.7

(adapted from *Roget's International Thesaurus*, fourth edition)

1. The value of the stock *appreciated* during the time he owned it. _____

_____

2. Mark *appreciated* the seriousness of the problem. _____

_____

3. Maria's parents *appreciated* the flowers she sent for their anniversary. _____

_____

4. Tara *appreciated* good music. _____

_____

STUDY TIP: Once you find the synonyms in a thesaurus entry, try out each word in your sentence to decide which one conveys the meaning you want.

Doing Research from an Encyclopedia

The **encyclopedia** is a **reference book**. *Encyclopedia* means "course of general education" in Greek.

In a general encyclopedia, you will find short articles about people, places, animals, events, ideas, religions, and so on. A general encyclopedia, organized in alphabetical order, contains many volumes, usually twenty or more.

There are also one-volume encyclopedias with short entries on many subjects. You may find at the library special subject encyclopedias on art, education, religion, science, or biography.

When you have a topic to research:

■ Start by reading an encyclopedia article about it. The encyclopedia article is an overview of a topic. The article will give you ideas about what is important and what you might want to look into further.

■ At the end of the article, other related articles in the encyclopedia are listed.

■ There is often a bibliography or list of books to read on the topic. Some encyclopedias even have study questions and outlines of the longer articles.

General encyclopedias are updated every year. For the most up-to-date information, you should use the most recent edition.

Often, you can find the article simply by looking in the appropriate volume number. Articles are classified alphabetically. You can look up information about a famous person by looking for his or her last name. You can look up a country by looking under the first letter of its name. But for some topics, you can save time by looking in the index. Do this if you think the topic may be mentioned in several articles, or if it doesn't have its own separate article.

On the next page is a portion of the index from the *World Book* encyclopedia.

Artificial respiration A:761
  Asphyxiation A:816
  Drowning (Applying First Aid) D:352
  First Aid (Restoring Breathing) F:138
    with pictures
Artificial satellite See Satellite,
  Artificial in this index
Artificial silk See Rayon in this index
Artificial skin
  Skin Grafting S:496
Artificial snow
  Snow (Artificial Snow) S:540
Artificial sweetener A:761
  Saccharin S:4
Artificial turf A:761
Artificial valve [medicine]
  Heart (Fixing Defective Heart Valves) H:146
    with picture; (table) H:148
Artigas, José Gervasio [Uruguayan patriot] A:761
  Uruguay (Independence) U:245

Excerpted from *The World Book Encyclopedia.* © 1989 World Book, Inc. By permission of the publisher.

▶ In what volume of the encyclopedia would you find an article about artificial skin? ____

Answer: S

▶ Under what general article? _____

Answer: skin grafting

PRACTICE

Directions: Use the *World Book Encylopedia* index at the top of this page to answer these questions.

1. **a.** In what volume would you find an article about the artificial heart valve? ____ What page? ____
   b. Under what article is this topic included? _____

2. Under what general article is artificial snow discussed? _____

3. **a.** Who was José Gervasio Artigas? _____
   b. Under what article will you find him discussed? _____

4. **a.** Does artificial sweetener have its own separate entry? ____
   b. What related article is included in the encyclopedia? _____

5. **a.** In what volume and on what page will you find the article about artificial respiration? _____
   b. In what volume and on what page will you find a picture showing how to restore breathing through first-aid measures? _____

MORE PRACTICE

Directions: Read the following article from the *World Book Encyclopedia,* then answer the questions below.

Bunche, Ralph Johnson (1904–1971), was an American statesman. In 1950, he won the Nobel Peace Prize, the first awarded to a black. He was appointed to the United Nations Palestine Commission in 1947, and worked with Count Folke Bernadotte on the Arab-Israeli dispute. After Bernadotte was assassinated, Bunche carried on the negotiations and arranged an armistice in 1949 (see **Israel** [History]). He won the peace prize for this work.

   Bunche was considered an authority on problems of colonialism. He began his diplomatic career in 1944 when he joined the Department of State. Bunche served as an adviser or delegate to nine international conferences in four years. He helped lay the groundwork for the United Nations (UN), and, in 1946, became director of the division of trusteeships in the Secretariat. He was an undersecretary of the UN from 1955 to 1971.

   Bunche was born in Detroit. He worked his way through the University of California at Los Angeles, and was graduated in 1927. He received a Ph.D. from Harvard University in 1934. Bunche also studied in London and South Africa. He began teaching at Howard University in 1928. Bunche won the Spingarn Medal in 1949 (see **Spingarn Medal**). *Richard L. Watson, Jr.*
See also **United Nations** (The Arab-Israeli Wars).

Additional resources
Haskins, Jim. *Ralph Bunche: A Most Reluctant Hero*. Hawthorn, 1974. Suitable for younger readers.
Mann, Peggy. *Ralph Bunche: UN Peacemaker*. Coward, 1975.

Excerpted from *The World Book Encyclopedia.* © 1989 World Book, Inc. By permission of the publisher.

---

1. In what year was Bunche born? _____ When did he die? _____

2. What do you think was Bunche's claim to fame? _____

_____

3. What article (and subsection) in the encyclopedia will tell you more about Bunche's involvement in negotiating an armistice in Israel? _____

4. Name two other related articles listed in this entry.

_____

5. What is the name of the section that lists other books to read about Bunche?

_____

6. On what topic was Bunche considered an expert? _____

STUDY TIP: Pay special attention to the first sentence or two of an encyclopedia entry. It is usually a definition or summary statement about the significance of the person, place, or thing.

Researching Magazine Articles

To find listings of recent magazine articles, use the *Reader's Guide to Periodical Literature.* (*Periodical* is another word for magazine.) The guide lists articles from about 200 popular magazines. A list of those magazines is included at the front of the guide, which is issued twice a month. At the end of the year, all the information for that year is bound into a hardcover book.

There are also other guides with narrower focuses, such as the *Art Index, Business Periodicals Index,* and *New York Times Index* (which indexes only articles from that newspaper).

Articles in the periodical indexes are listed alphabetically by subject. Under the subject, they are listed alphabetically by title. The author's name follows the title. The abbreviation "il" tells you the article is illustrated. The title of the magazine is shown in *italic* type, followed by the volume number and page. The last piece of information is the date of the issue in which the article appears.

For example, if you looked up the subject of whales, you would have found the following listing in a recent issue of the *Reader's Guide to Periodical Literature.* As you can see, there are many abbreviations in the entries.

WHALES
See also Whaling

Cetacean prognosis. G. Stone. il *Oceans* 21:56–7 N/D '88
Free at last! Bon Voyage! [whales trapped in Alaskan ice] A. Dorfman. il
   Time 132:130 N 7 '88
Heading south [whales trapped in Alaska] M. Clark. il *Newsweek* 112:10
   N 7 '88
Helping out Putu, Siku and Kanik [international effort to rescue Whales
   trapped by Alaskan ice] E. Linden. il *Time* 132:76–7 O 31 '88
Heroic measures for gentle giants [efforts to free trapped gray whales
   from Alaska ice] *U.S. News and World Report* 105:12 O 31 '88
Just one mammal helping another [trying to save the whales in Alaska] J.
   Adler. il map *Newsweek* 112:74–5) O 31 '88
Looking at them looking at us [rescue of trapped gray whales in Alaska]
   R. Rosenblatt. il *U.S. News and World Report* 105:8–9 N 7 '88
Saving grays [trapped whales in Alaska] il *Life* 11:42–5 D '88
To save the whales [international efforts to free from ice in Alaska] J.S.
   Kunen. il *People Weekly* 30:60–2+ N 7 '88
Whales: an era of discovery. J. Darling. il maps *National Geographic*
   174:872–909 D '88
The whales of Alaska [trapped grey whales] N. Underwood. *Maclean's*
   101:46+ O 31 '88

WHALES, KILLER See Killer Whales

WHALES IN POETRY
Whale Nation. H. Williams. il *Oceans* 21:36–43 S/O '88

▶ Look at the entry listed under WHALES IN POETRY.

a. What is the article called? _____

b. Who wrote the article? _____

c. What is the name of the magazine in which it appears? _____

d. What volume was it in? _____ What pages? _____

e. What was the date of that issue of the magazine? _____

PRACTICE

Directions: Use the index on the previous page to answer these questions.

1. To find a complete listing of articles on killer whales, under what entry should you look? _____

2. a. In what magazine could you find the article "Cetacean Prognosis"? (*Cetacean* is another word for whale.) _____

   b. What month and year? _____

   c. On what page does the article begin? _____

3. What is the article "Saving Grays" about? _____

4. What is the name of the article about whaling that appeared in *Newsweek* in October 1988? _____

5. a. In what magazine was "Whales: an Era of Discovery" published?

   _____

   b. In what month was that article published? _____

6. Suppose you were looking for general articles about whales, rather than news articles about whales trapped in Alaska. Name the two magazines and their articles that you would try to find copies of.

   a. _____

   b. _____

STUDY TIP: When doing research, read the title and any explanations in brackets to decide if the article is relevant to you. Then ask the librarian to help you find the back issue of the magazine.

Using the Library

Books are shelved in the library according to their *call number*. Most libraries use the *Dewey decimal classification system* to assign call numbers. Books are numbered from 001 to 999. They are divided into ten major categories. For example, all books numbered from 900 to 999 are history and geography books.

Within the 900s, books are divided into ten smaller categories. For example, books in the 940s are about European history. Within the 940s, the books are divided into still narrower categories. Dewey decimal numbers look like this: 944.77. There may also be letters after the number. The letters stand for the author's last name.

Very large libraries use the *Library of Congress classification system*. It uses call numbers that begin with one or two letters. Those letters are followed by a number between 1 and 9999. There can also be decimal numbers added to it. The call number might look like this: LN953.77.

Card Catalog

To find out the number of the book you want, look in the card catalog. The card catalog can be in different forms. It may be:

- Small drawers with index cards

- Microfiche: The catalog cards are photographed on small sheets of microfilm. You look at them through a projector.

- A computer-based system. You type in what you are looking for on a keyboard and the information comes up on a screen.

No matter what system your library uses, the information in the catalog is the same. Books are filed alphabetically under three different categories:

- Author or editor (If there is more than one author or editor, there will be a card for each.)

- Title

- Subject (A book may be filed under more than one subject, but it always has the same call number.)

All three cards are the same, except for the first line. On a title card, the title is at the top. On a subject card, the subject is at the top. On an author card, the author's name is at the top.

If you know the author or the title of the book you want, you can look under either category in the card catalog. Titles and authors are filed alphabetically. One book is indexed on each card.

▶ Suppose you wanted to find a card for *The Barbarians* by Victor Lazzaro. What word in the title would you look for in the catalog to find the title card? _____

Answer: Barbarians

▶ What word would you look up to find the author card? _____

Answer: Lazzaro

PRACTICE

1. **Directions:** Put these three books in alphabetical order:
   The Barbarians, The Barbarian Invasions, Barbarian Invaders.

   _____, _____, _____

2. Put these authors' names in alphabetical order. Write their last names first.

   Jessamyn West   _____

   George Eliot   _____

   Taylor Caldwell   _____

   Lewis Carroll   _____

   Joyce Carol Oates   _____

   John Irving   _____

   James Baldwin   _____

   T. S. Eliot   _____

   Nathanael West   _____

Challenge

St. in the names *St. James* or *St. John* stands for Saint. Would you find those names filed under *Sa* or *St*?

Finding Subject Cards

If you don't know the names of any books on the topic you are researching, use the subject catalog. In many libraries, subject cards are filed separately from title and author cards.

Subjects are indexed alphabetically—by words. For example, *Greenland* is filed after *Green Mountain Boys*. If you don't find your topic right away, look a little further in the card catalog. Here is a typical subject card. The subject is listed at the top. Other cards the book is filed under are listed at the bottom.

```
              UNITED STATES--HISTORY--CIVIL WAR,
                 1861-1865--SOCIAL ASPECTS
    973.7
    Sut      Sutherland, Daniel E
             The expansion of everyday life,
           1860-1876 / Daniel E. Sutherland. New
           York : Harper & Row, 1989.
             290 p., [12] p. of plates : ill.

             Bibliography: p. [271]-280.
             Includes index.

             1. United States--Social life and
           customs--1865-1918.  2. United States--
           History--Civil War, 1961-1865--Social
           aspects. I. Title.

    E168.S957 1989                              973.7
    ISBN 0-06-016023-3                         88-45527
```

PRACTICE

Directions: Use the card above to answer these questions.

1. What is the author's name? _____

2. Under what subject did you find this card? _____

3. Under what other subject is this book filed?

_____

4. How many pages are in this book? _____

5. What is the copyright date? _____

6. What three special features does the card list for this book?

_____

When you look up subjects in the card catalog, you may have to do a bit of detective work to find your topic. If you don't find your topic, ask yourself if you are being too general—or too specific. Think of what other subject it might be listed under.

MORE PRACTICE

Directions: For each item below, what subject would you look up in the subject card catalog to find references? Since the catalog is in alphabetical order, write the word or phrase under which you would find the subject filed.

1. A book about the American artist Georgia O'Keeffe

_____

2. General information about the state of Vermont

_____

3. Books about the plays of William Shakespeare

_____

Suppose you looked up these exact terms in the subject catalog and couldn't find cards. What other categories might you look up to find discussion of these items?

4. Angora rabbits _____

5. Juneau, Alaska _____

6. Black soldiers of the American Revolution _____

7. The Indian elephant _____

8. Lunar eclipses _____

9. Hardwoods of the eastern United States _____

10. La Follette, leader of the Progressive Party _____

Finding a Book in the Stacks

The call number you found in the card catalog directs you to the books on the shelves (also called stacks). Books are divided into two large sections:

- ■ *Fiction* books (those works of the imagination made up by writers) are usually listed alphabetically according to the author's name. At the ends of the shelves are letters telling you what authors' books are there: *Bar-Daw, Daw-Ferg*.

- ■ *Nonfiction* books (those containing information that is not made up) are organized according to the Dewey decimal system or some other classification system. Find the shelf you are looking for by studying a library diagram or asking the librarian. At the ends of these shelves, there are also signs telling you what numbers are on those shelves. Books are shelved in numerical order.

J–M

Fiction books are organized alphabetically.

947–953.7

Nonfiction books are organized by the Dewey decimal system.

Reference Books

When you are at the library, you can use reference materials. Reference materials are shelved separately from other books. The Dewey decimal call number has an *R* in front of it. These materials can only be used in the library. You cannot take them home.

If you want to know the answer to a quick question, call the reference department of the library. Look in the phone book for the name of the library and ask for the *reference* department.

Librarians are there to help you find the books and information you need. Ask the librarian for help. If you need a book that has been checked out, ask the librarian to hold it for you or to put it "on reserve." When it is returned, the librarian will call you.

PRACTICE

Directions: For each call number below, decide whether or not you will find the book in the stacks listed next to it. Write *yes* or *no*.

	Call Number	Stacks	Yes or No		Call Number	Stacks	Yes or No
1.	973.45Cu	947–953.7	____	3.	015.2	001–150.0	____
2.	825.111De	825.1–875	____	4.	973.22Hen	973.5–999	____

STUDY TIP: After you have found the book's call number, go to the shelf you will find it on. Browse among the other books in those numbers too. You may find other related books of interest.

Chapter Review

Successful Student Checklist

Here are some things that can help you win at studying. Put a check ☑ in the box of each one that you do.

☐ You consult a dictionary when you need help spelling, hyphenating, or pronouncing a word.

☐ You try out each synonym in a thesaurus to decide which one has the exact meaning you want.

☐ You pay careful attention to the first sentence of an encyclopedia entry.

☐ When using the *Reader's Guide to Periodical Literature*, you read the title and any explanations to decide if the article is useful to you.

☐ You use the card catalog to help you find a book you need.

☐ You ask the librarian for help when you need to.

Comprehension Check

Guide Words

Directions: Write each of these words under the appropriate pair of guide words listed below:

bury, cab, buzz, Byzantine, bushel, bylaw

1. burst/businessman   **2.** buttress/byline   **3.** bypass/cabala

Word Meanings

Directions: Circle the letter of the best definition for the underlined word in each sentence.

1. Jill promised to <u>groom</u> the horses before she left.
   a. a person whose job is to tend, feed, and curry the horses
   b. to tend and curry
   c. to train for a job

2. George <u>assumed</u> that his parents would pay for dinner.
   a. to seize
   b. to take for granted
   c. to pretend

3. It takes one year for the earth to make a complete <u>revolution</u> around the sun.
   a. an overthrow of a government or system
   b. a complete or drastic change
   c. movement around a center point

Dictionary Review

Directions: Use this dictionary entry to answer the questions below.

re•lax (ri-laks'), **vt.** [ME *relaxen*, to loosen < L *relaxare* < *re-*, back + *laxare*, to loosen, widen < *laxus*, loose: see LAX] **1** to make looser, or less firm or tense [to *relax* one's grip] **2** to make less strict or severe; soften [to *relax* discipline] **3** to abate; reduce; slacken [to *relax* one's efforts] **4** to release from intense concentration, hard work, worry, etc.; give rest to [*relax* the mind] **5** to treat (tightly curled hair) with a chemical solution so as to loosen the curls.

(From *Webster's New World Dictionary,* p. 1133)

1. How many syllables does this word have? _____

2. Circle the syllable that is stressed when you say the word *relax*.　**re lax**

3. a. What Latin word can *relax* be traced to? _____

　b. What does the Latin word mean? _____

4. Write the number of the definition for each usage of the word *relax* in this sentence: As Doug (a)*relaxed* his mind, he (b)*relaxed* his grip on the steering wheel.

　a. ____　　**b.** ____

5. Based on the definition, write two synonyms for *relax* that are found in the entry. _____

Reader's Guide to Periodical Literature

The following questions are based on the entries from the *Reader's Guide* below:

WHEAT

Cultivation

Staff of life. T. Leonard. il *Organic Gardening* 35:46–52 D '88

Diseases and pests

Sowing gene-altered antifungal bacteria [pseudomonas resistant to wheat take-all disease] *Science News* 134:300 N 5 '88

WHEAT WEAVING

Weaving wheat [holiday wreath] il *Sunset* (central West edition) 181:98–9 N '88

1. a. In what magazine was the article "Staff of Life" published? _____

　b. In what month and year was it published? _____

2. What is the article "Weaving Wheat" about? _____

3. Are there illustrations in any of these articles? ____ If so, which articles?

_____

Using the Card Catalog

Directions: For each author or title, write the word you would look under in the card catalog.

1. *Profiles in Courage* _____

2. William Shakespeare _____

3. a book of poems by Robert Frost _____

4. *Children of the Sun* _____

5. *The Great Gatsby* _____

Call Numbers

Directions: Decide whether each number is a Dewey decimal or Library of Congress call number. Write *DD* or *LC.*

_____ **1.** LC678

_____ **2.** 541.007 Kra

_____ **3.** 971.3

_____ **4.** K399.5

_____ **5.** 440.323 Ac

Chapter 6
Writing Research Papers

You've been assigned a paper to write on a subject of your choice. What do you do? How do you go about finding something to write, and then how do you execute it? Are there steps that you can follow to make this process easier? Chapter 6 will show you the steps involved in writing a paper, from coming up with an idea to organizing the parts that relate to the idea in some sensible form.

Words You'll Need to Know

These important words will be used in Chapter 6. Learn what each word means.

preliminary—introductory
bibliography—a listing of titles of books and articles used in research
brainstorming—writing down any idea that comes to mind when considering a topic
outline—a written plan showing the organization for a paper
spatial order—order determined by placement according to space
resource—an article or book that is consulted for information
refine—to make a broad subject narrower in focus

Following Writing Steps

When faced with the job of writing a research paper, you can follow these six steps to help you complete the task successfully:

- **Step 1. Choose a topic that interests you.** No matter what class your paper is for—science, history, geography, English—you *can* find a topic that is exciting to you. What are your hobbies and interests? Are you a musician? an athlete?

  Do some **brainstorming** to find a subject that you've always wanted to know more about. Enthusiasm about the subject will fire you up about doing the detective work to uncover interesting facts. When brainstorming, write down any ideas that come to you. Don't be self-critical; just write. You can always cross out ideas later.

- **Step 2. Do some preliminary reading.** Do preliminary reading to help you choose a topic or to decide if the topic you have chosen is a good one. Preliminary reading will also reveal to you what kinds of resources are available for your topic. Preliminary reading before doing in-depth research is like *previewing*. You will have an idea of what to expect when you research your paper. Read encyclopedia articles. Look through books in the library. Check tables of contents and indexes.

- **Step 3. Refine your topic.** Your paper should not be too broad or too narrow in scope. If it is too broad, it means that too much information is available for you to adequately write about the subject. If it is too narrow, it means that you will not find enough information to write about.

  For example, a paper on the subject of the American Civil War is too broad. However, there are many *aspects* to write about, such as the role of women in the Confederate and Union armies; the economy of the Confederacy, etc. A paper about the use of cannons in the Battle of Gettysburg is probably too narrow. Preliminary reading can help you refine your topic.

- **Step 4. When you choose a topic, think about the purpose of your paper.** In other words, what do you want to tell people? What is the main topic? What do you want to find out or prove through your research?

- **Step 5. Write down a few preliminary questions that you think your paper should answer.** You can come back to these questions later and change them.

- **Step 6. Use these questions as the basis for an outline for your paper.** Brainstorm for other questions and ideas that are related to your topic. Keep an open mind about your own ideas!

Sometimes after doing research, you may find that the topic is still too broad or too narrow for the number of pages you are to devote to the topic. However, you can still make some changes in your topic to make it more manageable to write about.

PRACTICE

Directions: For each pair of topics below, write B in front of the topic that is broader and N in front of the one that is narrower.

1. ____ **a.** how television portrays black people

   ____ **b.** the image of black people on "The Cosby Show"

2. ____ **a.** preventing heart disease through diet

   ____ **b.** how eating too many eggs can cause heart disease

3. ____ **a.** laser technology in surgery

   ____ **b.** new medical technology

4. ____ **a.** cultural trends in the U.S.

   ____ **b.** how music videos influence fashion

MORE PRACTICE

Directions: Choose a topic that you identified as narrow from the exercise above. Write three questions about that topic for which you want to find answers. For example, think about what you might ask an expert if you were doing an interview. If you find that you still haven't narrowed your subject enough, rewrite the topic until you are satisfied with it.

1. _____

2. _____

3. _____

STUDY TIP: After you have decided on a topic for your paper, write a one-paragraph summary of the paper. Write: "I will show that. . . . I will discuss these points. . . ." This will help you to focus your research.

Taking Notes with Note Cards

You'll find that writing your paper will be easier if you take notes on your **resource** materials.

Use three-by-five-inch index cards—or larger cards if your handwriting is large! Write one piece of information on each note card, so you can arrange the cards later to organize your topics. You will develop the notes into an outline and then write your paper in the order of the topics listed.

At the top of each note card, write a reminder that tells you which source the information is taken from. You can use the author's last name or a shortened version of the title. Look at the following example of how to fill out a note card:

Judo in the U.S.   Jones, p. 14

Hand-to-hand fighting is an American way of competing that combines wrestling and boxing. Very different from traditional judo.

STUDY TIP: Keep the information on your note cards brief. Include only *key* points.

Developing an Outline

In the lesson on page 91, you wrote out three questions that you might want to answer in a paper. Such questions and their subheads can form the outline for the paper. When you write note cards, you should write only one question or idea per note card. Later you will sort the questions or notes according to categories.

Here are examples of note cards used to develop the outline for the simple topic "How to Give a Speech." Notice how short the notes on each card are. Also notice that the categories or piles are in random order.

Pile 1
Characteristics
of a Speech

brevity - a speech should be only as long as necessary to get the point across

good enunciation - a speech should be understood; speaker should pronounce words correctly

eye contact - a good speaker maintains eye contact with the audience

spontaneity - a good speech sounds spontaneous - not "canned"

conclusion — wraps up speech; sums
up key points covered

body — the content or "meat"
of speech

introduction — introduces topic
and sets the tone

a speech can entertain the
audience

a speech can persuade; e.g. a
sales presentation, a campaign
rally

a speech can teach

a speech can inspire

Getting Organized

After you have taken notes for your paper, it's time to organize them. You have written an identification line on each card telling you what section of your paper the information belongs in. Classify the note cards by that identification line. Make separate piles for each section. Thumb through the cards. Do you want to change the categories at all? Do you want to move information from one pile to another? Look at your question and idea cards. In what pile does each of those belong? Which are most important and should be mentioned first? Which should be mentioned last? Are there any cards that are not useful? Put them aside. For some cards, there will be subheads.

Now it's time to use your index cards to help you write your **outline**. Generally, an outline includes the topic statement or title. The major headings under the title are identified by Roman numerals (I, II, III). Capital letters represent the supporting ideas that fall under the headings (A, B, C). Under the supporting ideas are details, which are identified by Arabic numbers (1, 2, 3). Some outlines even include subdetails that explain the details even further. These are identified by lower-case letters of the alphabet (a, b, c). By looking at your outline, you can see right away how a broad topic becomes narrower or more specific.

Most topics can be treated in a variety of ways. Your paper will probably fall into one of these patterns of organization: major issues or topics, degrees of importance, time order, or **spatial order**.

If you were doing a paper on native American crafts, you might organize it by one of the following categories:

Geographic Areas

- Eastern Woodlands
- Plains
- The Midwest
- Southeast
- Southwest
- Pacific Northwest

Type of Craft

- Pottery
- Basketry
- Weaving
- Metalwork

Other Major Issues

- The significance of the decorations
- The functional uses of native arts and crafts
- The ceremonial uses of selected implements
- The sale of native American crafts today—business or exploitation?

PRACTICE

Directions: Study the note cards on pages 93–94 about "How to Give a Speech." Then fill in the following outline using the notes on the cards. Be sure to think about the most effective order of the topics as you fill in the missing information.

How to Give a Speech

I. Purpose of a Speech

    A. _____

    B. _____

    C. _____

        1. _____

        2. _____

    D. _____

II. _____

    A. _____

    B. _____

    C. _____

III. _____

    A. _____

    B. _____

    C. _____

    D. _____

Completing Bibliography Cards

For each resource you use, complete a bibliography card. A **bibliography** is a listing of the materials you used for research. Write the complete information about the book: title, author, publisher, city where publisher is located, date of publication (copyright date). With these cards, writing a bibliography will be easy.

PRACTICE

Directions: Complete this bibliography card about a book you own or borrowed from the library:

Author (or editor) last name first:

Title of book:

Publisher:

Place where publisher is located:

Copyright date:

MORE PRACTICE

Directions: Write a bibliography card for one of the magazine articles in the *Reader's Guide to Periodical Literature* on page 79.

Name of the article:

Name of the author if given:

Name of the magazine:

Volume number, date of publication:

Pages article is on:

STUDY TIP: As an aid for organizing your topics, look at your resource books to see how their topics are ordered.

Chapter Review

Successful Student Checklist

Here are some things that can help you win at studying. Put a check ☑ in the box by each one that you do.

☐ In order to focus your research, you write a one-paragraph description telling what you will prove or discuss in your research paper.

☐ You use note cards to write down information from your sources when planning your paper.

☐ You develop an outline of your key topics and subtopics before you begin writing your paper.

Comprehension Check

Choosing a Topic

Directions: Write T for true or F for false for each statement below.

_____ **1.** Brainstorming can help you think of a topic for your paper.

_____ **2.** When you brainstorm, be careful to write down only the best ideas that are worth saving.

_____ **3.** Preliminary reading will help you discover what resources are available for your topic.

_____ **4.** Preliminary reading can help you refine your topic.

_____ **5.** If your topic is too narrow, you will have more resources than you can possibly handle.

_____ **6.** Questions you brainstorm for your topic can become the basis for your outline.

_____ **7.** Once you have decided on a topic and outline, you should not change it.

Bibliography Cards

Directions: Complete the information for the bibliography card for this book in the card catalog:

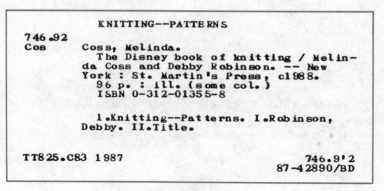

```
              KNITTING--PATTERNS
746.92
Cos       Coss, Melinda.
              The Disney book of knitting / Melin-
          da Coss and Debby Robinson. -- New
          York : St. Martin's Press, c1988.
              96 p. : ill. (some col.)
              ISBN 0-312-01355-8

              1.Knitting--Patterns. I.Robinson,
          Debby. II.Title.

TT825.C83 1987                        746.9'2
                                  87-42890/BD
```

Title of book:

Authors:

Publisher:

Location of Publisher:

Copyright date:

Taking Notes

Directions: For the paragraph below, write two note cards for a paper on impeachment.

The seventeenth president of the United States, Andrew Johnson, was impeached for violation of the Tenure of Office Act, improper use of his veto power, and other crimes. His trial, which lasted more than two months, began on March 13, 1868. Johnson was dangerously close to being convicted. Thirty-five senators voted "guilty," but that was one vote short of the two-thirds majority needed to convict him.

Chapter 7

A Winning Attitude

It's natural to be nervous about taking tests. Tests are a challenge. Even the boldest adventurers get nervous and scared before their next challenge, whether it is parachuting from a plane or climbing a mountain. But challenges help us to grow and learn. A positive attitude will help you learn the best material and perform at your best.

Your next test can be an opportunity for you to challenge yourself.

Words You'll Need to Know

These important words will be used in Chapter 7. Learn what each word means.

absolute—a word that means without exception, such as *all, every, none,* etc.

qualifier—a word that limits or changes the meaning of another word, such as *most, many, some*

judgment—an opinion or expression of one's feeling about something

objective—not affected by one's personal feelings or opinion; fair

paraphrase—to write or explain something in your own words

cram—to study for a test at the last minute

Getting Ready

When you are preparing for a test, **start** studying the day the test is announced. If you study a little every day, you won't have to stay up late and **cram** the night before the test. It's important to get a good night's sleep before the exam so that you will be clear-headed for the test.

- Right before you go to bed, take a last look at the material. Don't try to memorize at that point; just make yourself more familiar with it; then go to bed. (We'll take a closer look at studying in the next lesson.)

- If you have a tough time getting ready for school in the mornings, get your clothes and books together *before* you go to bed. Get up early enough so that you don't have to rush to get to school. There's no sense in making yourself any more nervous or frantic by being late.

- Eat a healthy breakfast the day of the test. Remember: food is fuel.

PRACTICE

Directions: Review the introduction to Chapter 1 called "Getting Motivated" on pages 2 and 3.

Write a positive statement to recite to yourself as you prepare for tests. Take into account your own goals and motivation when you write your statement. Here are a few suggestions for statements:

- "As I study and review, I feel more and more confident about taking this test."

- "I feel good about taking this test because I am prepared."

- "I am excited about learning."

STUDY TIP: For extra motivation, set a goal to reach for on your next test. Don't make your goal too easy or too hard to achieve. Decide on an appropriate reward for achieving your goal. Your reward should be something you are sure you can have or afford.

Studying for a Test

Do you review your notes even when you aren't having a test? It's a good idea to do it, though many of us don't. So preparing for a test provides a good opportunity to make sure we know the material before we move on to a new chapter or unit.

If you have been putting some of the lessons in this book into practice, you have already made progress toward doing well on your next test. You have been learning about how to study. Many of the techniques you have already learned in this book will come in handy when you study for a test. You will probably want to review each of those lessons.

SQ3R

Do you remember the SQ3R method of studying? SQ3R stands for survey, question, read, recite, review. (Reread the lesson on pages 50–51.) You can use this technique for studying for a test.

1. **Survey the material as a first step in test preparation.** Reacquaint yourself with the material by reading introductions, summaries, headings, and study questions. You can also use the previewing technique (page 43) as an early step in test preparation. This technique involves reading

   - the first paragraph or two of each chapter

   - the first two sentences of the middle paragraphs

   - the last paragraph or two of each chapter

   Using these surveying techniques for review will give you a good idea of what you already remember and understand and what you need to study in more detail.

2. **Then test your knowledge by using the *question* technique.** Turn each heading into a question. Close your book and see if you can answer the question. If you can't, you will need to study that section carefully by reading, then reciting the information.

3. **The night before the test, *review* briefly using previewing techniques.**

Study Your Notes

Review notes you took in class and notes you made when you read your textbook. Your notes highlighted the most important information and ideas. If you didn't take notes when you read, take some as you study for your test. The act of writing down the information will help you remember it. Note taking is also a way of reciting the information.

Review your homework assignments. Test yourself by answering the questions again. Pay particular attention to any questions you missed. If you are studying for a math test, do the problems again. Cover up the answers.

Did you write down questions your teacher asked in class? Pay attention to those class notes and the information that your teacher emphasized.

Memory Aids

If the test is on spelling, vocabulary, or a foreign language, review with flash cards. If the test will be short-answer or factual, ask a friend or family member to quiz you. Or study with a classmate and quiz each other.

Use memory aids you learned about (see pages 56–57) for formulas and lists of names and dates.

PRACTICE

Directions: Write T for true or F for false for each of the statements below.

_____ **1.** SQ3R is a method of studying for tests or reading class assignments.

_____ **2.** Flash cards are useless unless you use them with a partner.

_____ **3.** Two ways of studying for tests are previewing and reviewing class notes.

_____ **4.** You can test yourself by turning subheads into questions and then answering the questions.

_____ **5.** The best time to start studying for a test is the night before.

Challenge

You have been *taking* tests for years. Now here's your chance to make up your own test. Make up a test for the chapter you have just completed in social studies, science, math, or some other subject. Use other tests as models for writing this one. Wait a day or two, then take the test yourself to help you review. How did you do on your own test? You could also give the test to other students in that class.

STUDY TIP: Use tests you have already taken in the course to help you prepare for the next test. Note the kinds of questions the teacher likes to ask. Note the kinds of questions you did well on and what areas need extra study.

Starting the Test

1. **Skim through the entire test first.** When the teacher hands out the test, skim it before you start answering any questions. Get a good idea of what the format of the test is and what kind of questions you are being asked. Then plot your strategy by answering the following questions:

   • How much time will you spend on each section?

   • What sections count most?

   • Is there an essay question that will require a lot of time?

   • What section will you start on?

   • Where will you go from there?

   Remember to allow five to ten minutes at the end of the test for checking your answers.

2. **Follow directions.** Read the directions carefully. Even if you think you have seen those same instructions hundreds of times before, read them anyway. Be sure you know what you are being asked to do. If you are not sure, ask the teacher!

3. **Answer the easiest questions first.** For most tests, it doesn't matter in what order you answer the questions. So answer the easiest questions first. By doing this, you will increase your confidence. You will also trigger your memory. Once you get warmed up (and calmed down), other information will come to you. You'll be amazed at how much you actually remember.

   After you have answered all the questions you are fairly sure about, go back to the more difficult ones.

   Should you guess if you're not sure of an answer? There's always a chance you'll write down the correct answer. In the next few lessons, we'll look at ways of figuring out what the answer might be.

4. **Stay alert.** Deep breathing helps calm you down if you feel nervous. If your hand gets tired, shake it for a few seconds. Think positive thoughts as you take the test. If you don't know an answer, don't linger over it. Go on to the next question.

5. **Check your answers.** Check your answers when you are finished. Make sure you didn't make any careless mistakes. Did you write F where you meant to write T? Did you circle *a* when you meant to circle *c*? Make sure that your answers are legible. If you crossed out and corrected an answer, will the teacher be able to read the new answer? If you were taking a math test, did you make any careless errors in computation? Check your calculations.

Be careful about changing too many of your answers at this point, though. Change your answer only if you have rechecked it carefully. Very often, your first answer is the correct answer.

PRACTICE

Directions: Match the correct ending with the statement.

_____ **1.** Skim the entire test carefully,

_____ **2.** To increase your confidence,

_____ **3.** Even if you have seen them before,

_____ **4.** Don't change your answers

_____ **5.** If you don't know the answer to a question,

a. read the directions carefully.

b. unless you have checked them carefully.

c. go on to the next one.

d. before you start the test.

e. answer the easiest questions first.

STUDY TIP: If you're stumped by a question, move to another. Don't get bogged down on one question early in the exam. Answer the other questions, and then go back to the difficult questions.

Answering True-False Questions

You have probably answered a lot of **_true-false_** questions over the years. That's because they are a good way to measure your factual knowledge and your understanding.

As you know, in a true-false exercise, you must decide whether or not a statement is correct. Instructions may vary. You may have to circle T or F or write the letter in a blank.

Here are some clues to look for when you complete a true-false test or exercise.

■ Absolutes

Absolutes include words such as *all, nothing, always, never, completely, forever, every, none,* and so on.

An absolute in a statement is a signal to think carefully about whether there are ever any exceptions to the statement. If there is an absolute in a statement, ask yourself, "Are there ever any times when this would not be true?" For practice, complete the short activity below.

► Circle T or F:

T   F   A statement that has an absolute in it is *always* false.

You should have circled F for false. The word that signals the absolute is *always.* A statement with an absolute in it is *very often* false. However, there are exceptions. Consider this example:

► Circle T or F:

T   F   In geometry, a square *always* has four 90-degree corners.

In this case, the absolute is true. You can figure out the correct response by asking yourself whether it is possible for a square to have four corners that are not 90-degrees each.

■ Qualifiers

The words *most, many, often, usually,* and other such words are **qualifiers**. They are often signals that a general sweeping statement is being modified.

■ Judgments

Statements that make **judgments** are often false, unless you are being asked for your *opinion*. In an earlier lesson, there was a true-false statement that read:

> Flash cards are *useless* unless you use them with a partner.

106

The word *useless* is a judgment or opinion—and an absolute. Statements that express an opinion are likely to be false.

■ **One word can make the difference.** Focus on proper nouns, dates, and other key words or definitions. Everything might be correct except one key word.

▶ In some true-false exercises, you must supply the correct word or phrase to make a false statement true. Here is an example:

T F Albany is the capital of the United States.

Answer: False; Washington, D.C., is the capital of the United States.

PRACTICE

Directions: Write T for true or F for false next to each statement below.

_____ **1.** An absolute statement is always true.

_____ **2.** Most high school students do not attend school in the summer.

_____ **3.** All cars run on gasoline.

Circle T or F for each statement below.

T F 4. Teenagers of today completely reject their parents' values.

T F 5. As of 1990, there had never been a female president of the United States.

MORE PRACTICE

Directions: Write T for true or F for false. If the statement is false, correct the *italicized* word or words to make the statement true. Write the correction above the *italicized* words.

_____ **1.** *Circle graphs* are often used to show how budgets are spent.

_____ **2.** An *encyclopedia* is a book of synonyms.

_____ **3.** An *index* is an alphabetical listing of the topics in a book.

_____ **4.** The *Reader's Guide to Periodical Literature* directs you to reference books.

_____ **5.** The library's card catalog directs you to *books*.

STUDY TIP: Sometimes it helps to turn a true-false statement into a question. If you can answer *yes* to it, it is true. If you can answer *no* to it, it is false.

Answering Multiple-Choice Questions

Multiple-choice questions test your memory of factual information, your comprehension, or your ability to interpret information. Multiple choice may be used for math, social studies, science, reading, or vocabulary testing.

Read the directions carefully to find out how you are to indicate the correct answer. Be sure you put your answer in the correct space so that your teacher will see it when he or she grades your test.

A multiple-choice format may *ask a question* or ask you to *complete a sentence*. You are given three, four, or five possible answers from which to choose.

▶ Here's an example of a multiple-choice question:

Who was the second U.S. president?

a. Thomas Jefferson
b. John Adams
c. George Washington
d. Thomas Edison

You can narrow your choices by eliminating the answers that you *know* are wrong. George Washington was the first president. Edison was an inventor, not a president. That leaves choices *a* and *b*. If you had just studied early United States history, you might easily remember that Adams (*b*) was the second president and Jefferson was the third president. But even if you weren't sure in which order they served, you would now have a fifty-fifty chance of being correct even if you guessed between the two.

A multiple-choice format may ask you to draw conclusions or recognize the main idea, or even to bring in some background knowledge.

▶ Circle the letter of the statement that best expresses the main idea of this paragraph:

> The president of the United States has the right to appoint a Supreme Court justice when there is a vacancy. The Congress, however, must approve the president's choice. In fact, Congress has turned down some candidates for the Supreme Court.

a. There is a system of checks and balances in the selection of Supreme Court justices.

b. The Chief Justice of the Supreme Court has no voice in the selection of other justices.

c. A Supreme Court justice has a huge influence on court decisions long after the president who appointed him or her has left office.

Answer: Both *b* and *c* are true statements. But they do not address the content of the paragraph as *a* does.

There are some special types of multiple-choice questions to watch for when you read the directions. Some types of questions ask you to decide which answer is *wrong*. You may be given a group of words and be asked to decide which word does *not* belong. Here's an example:

▶ Write in the blank the letter of the word that does *not* belong in this group:

_____   **a.** heart   **b.** liver   **c.** stomach   **d.** spine

Answer: *d*; all of the rest are organs in the body.

PRACTICE

Directions: Read this short article, then answer each multiple-choice question on page 110. Circle the letter of the best answer.

The Supertrain

Can you imagine traveling up to 300 miles per hour on a train that can run alongside the interstate highways? Imagine how slow the cars on the highway would seem at fifty-five miles per hour. A panel of experts is recommending that the United States build such supertrains to answer many of the nation's transportation problems. These supertrains could replace many airplane flights, ease overcrowding of airports, and reduce air pollution by cutting down on gasoline use. The U.S. transportation secretary says that these trains have great potential.

The technology is called magnetic levitation, or *maglev* for short. It uses superconducting magnets to speed trains along a cushion of air on a guideway rail. Magnets in the guideway pull on magnets in the train. Electricity generates alternating north-south magnetic fields to coils along the guideway. Superconducting magnets on the train are attracted and repelled by the guideway magnets, thus moving the train along.

You can get an idea of the strength of a magnetic pull if you have two magnets. Hold south pole to south pole or north pole to north pole, and the magnets repel each other. Hold north to south pole, and the magnets attract each other. Notice the energy between the two magnets as they attract and repel.

---

1. According to the article, the maglev supertrain is propelled by
    a. the interaction between magnets on the train and magnets on the guideway rail.
    b. the magnetic pull of the guideway's south poles against its north poles.
    c. the pull of stronger magnets on the train against the pull of weaker magnets on the rail.

2. About how many hours would it take a maglev train traveling at maximum speed to go from Chicago to San Francisco (about 2,100 miles)?
    a. thirty-eight
    b. six and a half
    c. nine
    d. seven

3. Based on the article above, choose the best prediction.
    a. Planes and cars will become obsolete in the twenty-first century.
    b. Trains will become a high-speed means of travel and commerce in the twenty-first century.
    c. People will travel more in the twenty-first century.

STUDY TIP: When answering multiple-choice questions, try to determine the correct answer yourself *before* you look at the list of possible answers. Then look for your answer among the possible answers.

Taking Matching Tests

Matching exercises often test your understanding of vocabulary words. For many people, it is easiest to start with the word (usually in the left-hand column) and find the definition or best description in the right-hand list. If you are having a hard time, try doing it in the opposite manner to jog your memory and your reasoning skills.

After you have decided which column to begin with, look at only one item at a time in that column. Then look through the other column for the best answer.

Sometimes more than one answer may fit a word. Then you have to use a process of elimination. Does the definition fit any of the other words?

Maybe one item has you stumped. Do the other items first. If there is only one item left, there is your answer.

Be sure to note in the directions if there are the same number of items in each column or whether there are extra items in one of the lists.

PRACTICE

Directions: Match each term in column **A** with its definition in column **B**. Write the correct letter in the blank. Be careful: there are more definitions in column **B** than there are items in column **A**.

A	B
____ **1.** circle graph	**a.** compares two or more sets of information
____ **2.** bar graph	**b.** shows highs and lows over time
____ **3.** time line	**c.** is cut into pieces that add up to 100 percent
____ **4.** line graph	**d.** shows location, direction, and distance
____ **5.** map	**e.** shows chronology
	f. consists of lists of information

> **S**TUDY TIP: On a matching test, to avoid being distracted by other items, use your hand or a piece of scrap paper to cover up all but the item you are working on in the left-hand column. Lightly cross out any answer you have already chosen from the right-hand column.

Fill-in-the-Blank Questions

Some test items ask you to supply information. You must rely on your own memory rather than recognize the correct information on a multiple-choice list. These are called *fill-in-the-blank questions*. If you are answering such questions, read the directions carefully to see whether or not you must answer with complete sentences.

Here are some hints for recalling information for fill-in-the-blank items:

- Did any of the previous questions give you clues?

- What kind of answer must you provide? Read the context of the questions. Are you being asked for a noun? a verb? a person? a place? a date?

- In a fill-in-the-blank item, is there any clue that tells you whether the answer begins with a vowel or a consonant? The word *an* signals that the next word will begin with a vowel. The word *a* signals that the next word will begin with a consonant.

- Let the key word or phrase in the statement jump out at you, then try to make some associations with that word or name. What do you remember about that person or event? Does any of that information fit in the context of the sentence?

- If you are searching for a vocabulary term, think of the list of words you learned. Picture the words with their definitions.

PRACTICE

Directions: Read the hints for answering short-answer questions above. Then answer each question by filling in the blanks in each statement below.

1. A _____ is a reference book with word definitions, pronunciation guides, and word origins.

2. An _____ is a collection of books with articles on thousands of subjects.

3. To get a quick idea of what is in a chapter, you can _____ it.

Write a one- or two-word answer for each question.

4. What kind of book lists synonyms? _____

5. What kind of graph most readily shows highs and lows and changes over time? _____

Write a one-sentence answer for each question.

6. Define *glossary*. _____

_____

7. Name three ways in which library books are classified in the card catalog. ___

_____

_____

8. Tell what type of information circle graphs are often used to represent. _____

_____

9. Define *index*. _____

_____

10. Tell how books of fiction are shelved in a library. _____

_____

STUDY TIP: To answer fill-in-the-blank questions in which one word is missing, try plugging in possible answers. Then read the sentence aloud to determine whether the choice makes sense.

Planning for Essay Tests

An *essay* test gives you the opportunity to tell what you know and perhaps to even present your opinions. But you must back up your opinions with sound arguments and facts that you have learned in your reading, in research, or in class.

 Always read the directions carefully. Is there a time limit? Do the instructions say how many points the question is worth? Do you have a choice of questions? Or must you answer all of the essay questions? Do the directions say how long the answer should be or how many reasons you must give to support your opinion?

Follow these steps to answer an essay question:

■ **As you read each essay question, note the key words that tell you what to do.**

"*Why* did the United States decide to use an atomic bomb on Japan to end World War II? *Do you think* these reasons *justified* the use of the bomb? *Explain your reasons.*"

■ **Then paraphrase the question (write it in your own words).**

There are two parts to the question above. The first part starts with *why*: "Tell the reasons for the U.S. decision to use the atomic bomb." The second part asks for *your* opinion: "Do you think America's reasons for using the bomb were *good enough reasons* to use an atomic bomb? Back up your opinion." (You cannot simply answer yes or no.)

Here are some verbs that are often used in essay questions:

compare and contrast—explain the similarities and differences between two or more items
discuss—to investigate by reason or argument
trace—show the steps in a process or how an event developed
define—explain the meaning of a word or idea
explain—tell how or why
name or list—make a brief list

■ **Jot down notes and make a quick outline on the back of the test or on a piece of scrap paper.**

As soon as you read and understand the question, write down the words and ideas that come into your mind. That way you won't forget any of your first good ideas. And as you write down ideas, more ideas will come to you.

PRACTICE

Directions: Circle the key words in each essay question. Then paraphrase what each of these questions is asking.

1. Name four U.S. presidents who died while still in office, and briefly explain the circumstances of their deaths. _____

   _____

2. Do you think the death penalty is ever justified? If so, for what crimes should it be put into practice? Is there an alternative? Defend your opinion.

   _____

   _____

   _____

   _____

3. Discuss how the building of a maglev supertrain (on page 109) system would affect transportation and the environment in the United States.

   _____

   _____

MORE PRACTICE

Directions: Look at question 3 above about the maglev train. This is based on the passage you read on page 109. Jot down the words and ideas that come to mind as a response. If it helps, write *maglev* in the center of the page and write words around it as they come to you. This exercise calls on you to make some predictions based on your knowledge of transportation and the environment.

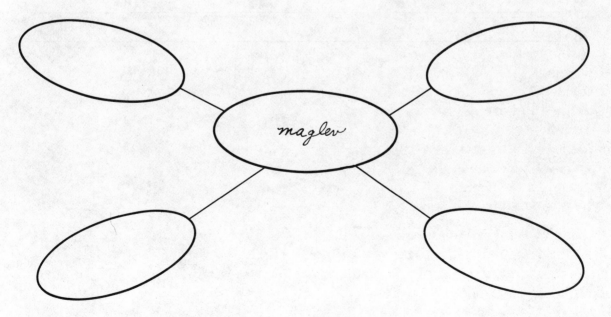

Now put those ideas into brief outline form. Notice that the question asks you to discuss *two* different areas that would be affected by the building of the maglev system. First brainstorm some general ideas like the ones in the idea box below, then the outline will practically write itself!

Idea Box

Transportation
personal travel
movement of freight
airplanes
cars

Environment
air pollution
noise pollution
landscape

I. Transportation

   A. _____

   B. _____

   C. _____

   D. _____

   E. _____

II. Environment

   A. _____

   B. _____

   C. _____

   D. _____

   E. _____

Answering Essay Test Questions

Now that you have planned your essay, you are ready to begin writing it.

■ **Write your answer in complete sentences and paragraphs. Develop an essay with three parts: an introduction, a body, and a conclusion.**

In your introduction, get right to the point: what is your position? Write a short introductory paragraph telling what you are going to prove in your essay. This is a preview of what is to come.

PRACTICE

Directions: Write an introductory paragraph for your essay about the maglev system. Include a short explanation of what the maglev train is, as well as a brief statement about what you are going to prove in your essay. You might base your essay on the points enclosed in the idea box below.

Idea Box

- The supertrain will have a great effect on the environment.

- The supertrain will have a great effect on transportation.

- The supertrain will have little effect on either the environment or transportation.

- The supertrain will affect transportation but not the environment.

_____

_____

_____

_____

_____

_____

_____

_____

Directions: Now write the body of the essay. This is where you will develop your ideas. Make a sound case for the opinion that you introduced in the first paragraph. Use all the relevant facts and information you can think of to back up your opinion.

In the space below, develop the ideas you included in your outline on page 116. Write one to two paragraphs on each area (transportation and the environment).

Transportation

_____

_____

_____

_____

_____

_____

_____

_____

_____

Environment

_____

_____

_____

_____

_____

_____

_____

_____

_____

Directions: Now write a brief conclusion for your essay. Summarize your argument in one paragraph.

_____

_____

_____

_____

_____

_____

_____

_____

_____

_____

■ **Reread your essay.** Be sure you leave time to reread your essay. Check to see that your essay is to the point and that you included all the ideas you intended to include. Also check for correct spelling, punctuation, and grammar.

Make any necessary corrections, but make them neatly. If you run out of time on an essay, outline the rest of your answer and hand that in. If your teacher sees that you knew the material but ran out of time, you may get partial credit.

STUDY TIP: In answering an essay question, pretend you are speaking to another person. Be sure to use proper grammar and sentence structure, however. Assume that the other person knows very little about the subject.

The Successful Student: Cramming vs. Studying

Have you ever tried to *cram* a shirt into a messy drawer? Did the drawer close? Or did it get stuck once you got it closed? Have you ever tried to *cram* another dish into a full refrigerator? Did the door close? The next time you opened that door, could you get the juice out without dishes of leftovers and a head of lettuce falling out onto the floor?

Now think about *cramming* for a test. That's right—it's the very same word. You are cramming or stuffing information into your head. But when you need to retrieve that information, will the drawer be stuck? Will you be able to get the information you need without a lot of other unnecessary information falling out too?

It's a lot easier to put things away and take them out if we keep that drawer or refrigerator organized. The same is true of studying. If you study regularly, you will be filing information away so that you can easily get at it when you have a test. Information won't be overflowing haphazardly.

This book has been all about studying and keeping up with schoolwork. By following some of the advice in this book, you can avoid cramming. By studying regularly, you use your memory efficiently and store information in your long-term memory. Then when you study for a test, you are reviewing information and recalling it from your memory, rather than trying to learn it for the first time.

Chapter Review

Successful Student Checklist

Here are some things that can help you win at studying. Put a check ☑ in the box by each one that you do.

☐ You start studying the day that a test is announced.

☐ You get a good night's sleep before the day of the test.

☐ You set a goal to reach on your next test, and reward yourself upon reaching it.

☐ You use tests you've already taken in a course to prepare for your next test.

☐ You carefully read test directions and ask the teacher to clarify any that might confuse you.

☐ If you're stumped by a question, you go on to the next one.

Comprehension Check

A Winning Attitude

Directions: Write a one-paragraph description of a winning attitude in studying. Use these words in your answer: *confidence, challenge, opportunity, test, study.*

_____

_____

_____

_____

_____

Taking Tests

Directions: Answer these questions using complete sentences.

1. Why is note taking an effective part of studying for a test?

_____

_____

2. What questions should you answer first on a test?

_____

_____

3. a. Write an example of an absolute statement that is false.

_____

b. Write an example of an absolute statement that is true.

_____

Fill in the Blanks

Directions: Use these words to fill in the blanks in the statements below: *eliminate, survey, recite, absolutes, qualifiers.*

1. *Always, never,* and *all* are examples of _____.

2. If you don't readily know the answer to a multiple-choice question, first

_____ the wrong answers.

3. Note taking is one way to _____ information after you have read it.

4. *Often, many,* or *some* are examples of _____.

5. _____ the material by reading introductions, summaries, headings, and study questions.

Essay Questions

Directions: Put the steps for answering an essay question in the proper sequence by numbering them from 1 to 7.

____ **a.** Write a conclusion.

____ **b.** Write the body of the essay.

____ **c.** Note the key words in the question.

____ **d.** Write a brief outline.

____ **e.** Write an introductory paragraph.

____ **f.** Reread the essay and make necessary corrections.

____ **g.** Jot down ideas.

Answer Key

Chapter 1: Getting Motivated

Getting in Shape
page 4
Answers will vary.

Chapter Review
page 8
1. **a** and **b**
2. **d**
3. **c**
4. **a**
5. **a** and **b**

Chapter 2: Using Textbooks

Using the Table of Contents
page 10
1. "What Is a Clown?"
2. page 22
3. page 45
4. Chapter 1, "What Is a Clown?"
5. Chapter 3; page 45

Locating Chapter Heads and Subheads
page 11
Answers will vary.

Finding Key Words and the Glossary
pages 12–13
Practice
1. A *jury* is a group of citizens who give a verdict in court.
2. A *subpoena* requires a person to appear in court to testify; a *summons* orders a person to appear in court but not necessarily to testify.
3. A *felony* is a major crime; a *misdemeanor* is a minor crime.
4. The defendant and the plaintiff oppose one another in a lawsuit.

More Practice
Your answers should be similar to these:
1. **bail**—money paid to the court to release a defendant from jail until the trial is over
2. **subpoena**—a written order telling a person to appear in court to testify;

testify—to tell what you know about a case in court
3. **acquit**—to find the defendant not guilty of a crime
4. **prosecute**—to carry out a case against a defendant

Understanding an Index
pages 14–15
Practice
1. pages 45 and 51
2. pages 45 and 52
3. page 99; cathrode ray tube
4. no
5. yes; no

More Practice
1. Roosevelt
2. United States or U.S.A.
3. Russia or Soviet Union or U.S.S.R.
4. Transportation
5. Supreme Court or Court
6. United Nations or U.N.
7. World War II
8. Jackson
9. Pearl or Pearl Harbor
10. elephants
11. Empire
12. Lucy

Using Introductions, Summaries, and Study Questions
pages 16–17
Practice
You should have checked **a, c, f, h**, and **i**.

Do It Yourself
Answers will vary.

Chapter Review
pages 18–19
Finding Your Way
1, 2, 4, 3, 5

Table of Contents
1. Chapter 6
2. Chapter 2
3. Chapter 3
4. Chapter 2

Index
1. page 112
2. Riser
3. pages 191–192
4. Insulation

5. Windows

6. Ventilation, vise grips, grains of woods

7. 190–191

8. 191–192

Chapter 3: Reading Visual Aids

Reading Bar Graphs
pages 21-23

Practice

1. California, New York, Texas, Florida, Illinois

2. Texas; Texas

3. yes; Illinois and Florida switched places

4. California

5. Illinois

More Practice

1. 1960, 1970, 1975, 1980, and 1987

2. a. women

   b. men

3. the number of people living alone—in millions; the years for which information is available

4. a. up

   b. up

5. no

6. a. between 11,000,000 and 12,000,000

   b. about 7,000,000

Challenge

Women live longer than men, so there are more older women living alone.

Do It Yourself

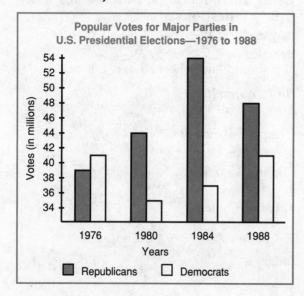

Popular Votes for Major Parties in U.S. Presidential Elections—1976 to 1988

Reading Line Graphs
pages 24-25

1. F   **4.** F

2. T   **5.** T

3. T   **6.** F

Reading Circle Graphs
pages 26-28

Practice

1. $638.5 billion.

2. American Financial Services Association.

3. a. 7%

   b. 1%

   c. 13%

   d. 23%

   e. 10%

4. a. commercial banks

   b. 46%

5. Gasoline companies

Challenge

Multiply the total ($638.5 billion) by the percent of the market share.

More Practice

1. the employment status of people 16 years old and older in the United States

2. 59.5%

3. a. 2,239,000

   b. 1.2%

4. 4%

5. 117,234,000

6. employed and unemployed

7. a. 64.3%

   b. 35.7% (34.5% + 1.2%)

Reading Charts
pages 29-31

Practice

1. 25,200

2. one year

3. Toyota

4. 120 points

5. Mazda and Audi

6. There was a tie for number nine.

Challenge

Imported cars outperform domestic cars.

More Practice

1. 81 degrees   **6.** 60%

2. 79 degrees   **7.** 30%

3. 90 degrees   **8.** 100%

4. 120 degrees   **9.** 70%

5. 72 degrees   **10.** 0%

Challenge
The higher the humidity, the *warmer* the temperature feels. The lower the humidity, the *cooler* the temperature feels.

Interpreting Maps
pages 32–33

1.

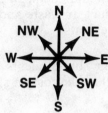

2. **a.** SW
   b. Central
   c. S
3. West
4. Northeast
5. Southeast
6. Superior, Ontario, Huron, Erie, Michigan
7. 600 miles

Challenge
Answers will vary.

More on Interpreting Maps
page 34

1. the Appalachian Mountains
2. Mississippi River
3. mountains
4. the Rocky Mountains

Reading Time Lines
pages 35–36

Practice

a. 9	**e.** 6	**i.** 10
b. 2	**f.** 7	**j.** 8
c. 11	**g.** 1	**k.** 12
d. 5	**h.** 4	**l.** 3

More Practice

1. 10
2. Democratic
3. Woodrow Wilson
4. Theodore Roosevelt
5. Thomas R. Marshall
6. Theodore Roosevelt
7. 50 years

Understanding Editorial Cartoons
pages 37–39

Practice

1. USAF Turkey Farm
2. United States Air Force

3. the slang term; a failure or flop
4. B-2 bomber
5. money; it costs too much
6. The B-1 bomber is a failure, and it is costing too much money to keep it going.

More Practice
The waters are becoming so polluted that the fish can't breathe or survive.

Chapter Review
pages 40–41

Graphs and Charts

1. circle	**5.** chart
2. bar	**6.** chart
3. line	**7.** chart or bar
4. circle	**8.** line

Map Skills

1. scale	**3.** legend
2. compass	

Time Lines

1. F	**3.** T
2. T	**4.** F

Editorial Cartoons

1. d	**6.** c
2. a	**7.** g
3. b	**8.** f
4. h	**9.** i
5. e	

Chapter 4: Reading Strategies

Previewing
pages 43–45

Practice

1. Hummingbirds are very active.
2. At night, hummingbirds sometimes go into a state of suspended animation called torpor.

More Practice
Your answers should be similar to these:

1. toothaches and how to diagnose them
2. Temporary pain is normal after a tooth has been filled.
3. Repeated bouts of pain can mean advanced dental decay.
4. Continuous pain plus fever could signal an abscess.
5. How to Diagnose a Toothache; or
   When to See a Dentist; or
   Reading Your Own Toothache Symptoms

Skimming
pages 46-47

Key words may vary.

Paragraph 2 main idea: Native Americans taught the early New England settlers how to extract the sweet sap from maple trees and boil it down into a sugary syrup. *Key words:* Native Americans taught, legend, Great Spirit.

Paragraph 3 main idea: Maple sugar farmers tap the trees by drilling a hole and inserting a spout called a tap. *Key words:* tap, drilling, Traditional, buckets, sugar shack.

Paragraph 4 main idea: The sap is boiled in a huge pot over a wood fire. *Key words:* boiled, wood fire, thin, forty gallons, one gallon.

Paragraph 5 main idea: Modern syrup producers have replaced the buckets with plastic tubing. *Key words:* Modern, plastic tubing.

Scanning
pages 48-49

1. **Answer:** China, Sumatra, and Java
2. **Keys:** How many, number
   Answer: 81
3. **Keys:** mean, word in italic type
   Answer: "worker" or "forced laborer"

Challenge
1. scan; you are looking for specific information
2. skim; you are looking for general information

Following the SQ3R Method
pages 50-51

Answers will vary but should be similar to these:
1. How did the Iroquois Confederacy influence the U.S. Constitution?
2. How does the television signal travel from the station to your home?
3. Who is the greatest leader of the twentieth century?

Note Taking
pages 52-53

Practice
Answers will vary.

More Practice
Answers will vary.

Drawing Thought Webs
pages 54-55

Practice
1. pollution
2. land, air, water, and radiation
3. acid rain and the greenhouse effect
4. trash disposal and chemical dumping
5. disposal of nuclear waste and risk of leaks and accidents

More Practice
Answers will vary, but students' thought webs should follow the format shown in this lesson.

Using Memory Aids
pages 56-57

Answers will vary.

Chapter Review
pages 59-60

Previewing

1. F	4. T
2. F	5. T
3. T	

Skimming and Scanning

1. scan	4. scan
2. skim	5. skim
3. skim	6. scan

SQ3R
Survey, Question, Read, Recite, Review

Note Taking

1. b	3. a
2. a	4. c

Memory Aids
Students can name any three memory aids: flash cards, note taking, catch words or phrases, repetition, reciting.

Listening
The following should be checked: 1, 2, 5

Chapter 5: Using Reference Tools

Putting Words in Alphabetical Order
pages 62-63

Practice

1. planetarium	7. relativity
2. plate	8. rhinoceros
3. pleasant	9. symmetry
4. pontiff	10. symphony
5. posthumous	11. synonym
6. receptacle	12. synthesis

More Practice

1. chimpanzee, China, chrome
2. humiliation, humming, hummingbird
3. diversity, dividend, divination
4. inhumane, iniquity, initiate
5. electrode, electromagnetic, electroscope
6. junior, juniper, junta
7. abacus, abashed, abate
8. sensation, sensible, sensuous
9. gadabout, gadfly, gadget
10. quarrel, quarry, quarter

Using Guide Words in the Dictionary
pages 64-65

Practice

1. miniscule	5. minister
2. miniseries	6. ministrant
3. miniskirt	7. ministration
4. ministate	8. ministry

More Practice

2. ahead	12. back
3. ahead	13. yes
4. back	14. back
5. yes	15. yes
6. back	16. ahead
7. yes	17. yes
8. ahead	18. back
9. ahead	19. yes
10. yes	20. ahead
11. back	

Improving Spelling and Hyphenation
pages 66-67

Practice

1. laboratory	6. February
2. OK	7. harass
3. OK	8. OK
4. diphtheria	9. misspell
5. bookkeeper	

More Practice

1. 3, self-centered
2. 2, deerskin
3. 3, deep-dish pie
4. 4, optimistic
5. 3, hobbyhorse
6. 3, Dixieland
7. 3, believing

Challenge

1. marsh•mal•low
2. tech•no•log•i•cal•ly
3. xy•lo•phone

Looking Up Word Meanings
page 68

1. conjunction	5. singular
2. plural	6. adverb
3. verb	7. noun
4. adjective	8. preposition

How Dictionaries Are Organized
pages 68-70

Practice

1. pamper	6. write
2. grip	7. woman
3. try	8. restore
4. loving or love	9. buy
5. wring	10. agree

More Practice

Answers will vary depending on the dictionary used but should be similar to these:

1. *adj.*, having or showing an excessively high regard for one's self, looks, etc.
2. *v.*, used up completely; emptied
3. *v.*, to uphold or defend; to declare to be true
4. *n.*, resentment or offense
5. *v.*, to bring to a specified state or condition
6. *n.*, an ornamental braiding for fastening the front of a garment
7. *n.*, business expenses not chargeable to a particular part of the work or product
8. *v.*, to make a full statement of one's taxable or dutiable property

Using Pronunciation Keys
page 71

The following syllables should be circled:

1. dine	7. ma
2. plan	8. tith
3. fed	9. nu
4. ul	10. mo
5. am	11. cel
6. trib	12. va

Looking Up Word Origins
page 72

Answers may vary depending on the dictionary used.

1. ME, *fon*—to act foolishly
2. L., *multus*—many; *plicare*—to fold
3. L., *in*—without; *somnus*—sleep
4. L., *ad*—to; *haerare*—stick

Choosing Words in a Thesaurus
pages 73-75
Practice
1. any three of these: rival, emulate, contend, strive, compete
2. any two of these: belief, appearance, vision, thought
3. neglect
4. contended, competed
5. panorama, vista, or scene

More Practice
1. increased 38.6. The value of the stock *increased* during the time he owned it.
2. understand 548.7; or know 475.12. Mark *understood* the seriousness of the problem.
3. be grateful 949.3. Maria's parents were *grateful* for the flowers she sent for their anniversary.
4. enjoy 865.10. Tara *enjoyed* good music.

Doing Research from an Encyclopedia
pages 76-78
Practice
1. **a.** H: 146
   b. Heart
2. Snow
3. **a.** Uruguayan patriot
   b. Uruguay
4. **a.** yes
   b. Saccharin
5. **a.** A: 761
   b. F: 138

More Practice
1. 1904; 1971
2. He was the first black person to win the Nobel Peace Prize.
3. Israel (History)
4. Springarn Medal and United Nations (Arab-Israeli Wars)
5. Additional resources
6. problems of colonialism

Researching Magazine Articles
pages 79-80
1. Whales, Killer
2. **a.** *Oceans*
   b. November–December 1988
   c. page 56
3. trapped whales in Alaska
4. "Just One Mammal Helping Another"

5. **a.** *National Geographic*
   b. December 1988
6. **a.** *Oceans*—"Cetacean Prognosis"
   b. *National Geographic*—"Whales: An Era of Discovery"

Using the Library
pages 81-82
1. *Barbarian Invaders, The Barbarian Invasions, The Barbarians*
2. Baldwin, James
   Caldwell, Taylor
   Carroll, Lewis
   Eliot, George
   Eliot, T. S.
   Irving, John
   Oates, Joyce Carol
   West, Jessamyn
   West, Nathanael

Challenge
Sa

Finding Subject Cards
pages 83-84
Practice
1. Daniel E. Sutherland
2. United States history—Civil War, 1861–1865—Social Aspects
3. United States—social life and customs
4. 290
5. 1989
6. illustrations, bibliography, and index

More Practice
1. O'Keeffe; or art
2. Vermont
3. Shakespeare
4. rabbits
5. Alaska
6. American Revolution; or blacks in the military
7. elephant
8. eclipse
9. hardwoods
10. Progressive Party

Finding a Book in the Stacks
pages 85-86
1. no
2. yes
3. yes
4. no

Chapter Review
pages 86–87

Guide Words
1. burst/businessman: bury, bushel
2. buttress/byline: buzz, bylaw
3. bypass/cabala: Byzantine, cab

Word Meanings
1. b
2. b
3. c

Dictionary Review
1. 2
2. lax
3. a. *relaxare*; or *laxus*
   b. to loosen
4. a. 4
   b. 1
5. Answers will vary.

The Reader's Guide to Periodical Literature
1. a. *Organic Gardening*
   b. December, 1988
2. holiday wreaths
3. yes; "Staff of Life" and "Weaving Wheat"

Using the Card Catalog
1. Profiles
2. Shakespeare
3. Frost
4. Children
5. Great

Call Numbers
1. LC
2. DD
3. DD
4. LC
5. DD

Chapter 6: Writing Research Papers

Following Writing Steps
pages 90–91

Practice
1. a. B
   b. N
2. a. B
   b. N
3. a. N
   b. B
4. a. B
   b. N

More Practice
Answers will vary.

Getting Organized
pages 95–96

   I. Purpose of a Speech
      A. to entertain
      B. to teach
      C. to persuade
         1. a sales presentation
         2. a campaign rally
      D. to inspire
  II. Organization
      A. introduction
      B. body
      C. conclusion
 III. Characteristics of a Speech
      A. brevity
      B. good enunciation
      C. eye contact
      D. spontaneity

Completing Bibliography Cards
page 97

Practice
Answers will vary.

More Practice
Answers will vary.

Chapter Review
pages 98–99

Choosing a Topic
1. T   5. F
2. F   6. T
3. T   7. F
4. T

Bibliography Cards
Title: *The Disney Book of Knitting*
Authors: Melinda Coss and Debby Robinson
Publisher: St. Martin's Press
Location of publisher: New York
Copyright date: 1988

Taking Notes
Answers will vary

Chapter 7: A Winning Attitude

Getting Ready
page 101
Answers will vary.

Studying for a Test
pages 102–103
1. T 4. T
2. F 5. F
3. T

Challenge
Answers will vary.

Starting the Test
pages 104–105
1. d 4. b
2. e 5. c
3. a

Answering True-False Questions
pages 107–108
Practice
1. F 4. F
2. T 5. T
3. F

More Practice
1. T
2. F; thesaurus
3. T
4. F; magazines (or periodicals)
5. T

Answering Multiple-Choice Questions
pages 108–110
1. a
2. d
3. b

Taking Matching Tests
page 111
1. c 4. b
2. a 5. d
3. e

Fill-in-the-Blank Questions
pages 112–113
1. dictionary
2. encyclopedia
3. preview or skim
4. thesaurus
5. line graph
6. A glossary is a list of a text's important words and their definitions.

7. Books are classified according to author, title, and subject.
8. Circle graphs are often used to represent how budgets are spent. They show how parts of a whole are divided.
9. An index is an alphabetical listing of the topics in a book.
10. Books of fiction are shelved alphabetically by the author's last name.

Planning for Essay Tests
pages 114–116
Practice
Answers will vary. Students should have circled these key words:
1. U.S. presidents who died while still in office
2. death penalty; justified; what crimes
3. maglev supertrain; affect transportation; environment

More Practice
Answers will vary.

Answering Essay Test Questions
pages 117–119
Answers will vary.

Chapter Review
pages 121–122
A Winning Attitude
Answers will vary.

Taking Tests
1. Note taking is a way of reciting information and the act of writing helps to store the information. Notes can also be used for later review.
2. Answer the questions that are easiest for you first.
3. Answers for *a* and *b* will vary.

Fill in the Blanks
1. absolutes
2. eliminate
3. recite
4. qualifiers
5. Survey

Essay Questions
6, 5, 1, 3, 4, 7, 2. *Note:* Some students may find it more efficient to write the body of the essay *before* the introduction.